GOD
WHO
LOVES

*The Promise and Privilege of
Knowing the Father*

The God Who Loves
© 2009 RBC Ministries

Discovery House Publishers is affiliated with
RBC Ministries, Grand Rapids, Michigan 49512

All rights reserved.

Cover Design: Stan Myers

Unless otherwise noted,
Scripture quotations are from
The HOLY BIBLE, NEW KING JAMES
VERSION, ©1979, 1980, 1982.
Used by permission of
Thomas Nelson, Inc., Publishers.

Printed in the United States of America
09 10 11 12 / 10 9 8 7 6 5 4 3 2 1

CONTENTS

PREFACE

In the 1960s, Jackie DeShannon sang "What the World Needs Now Is Love." It was a song that cried out for the one thing we hunger and thirst for most deeply—yet we often don't know where to find it. Perhaps this unsatisfied searching is because, as another song put it, we are "Looking for Love In All the Wrong Places." If we fail to look in the right places, we will never know the kind of love our hearts crave.

French mathematician and philosopher Blaise Pascal (1623-1662) wrote of this problem in his theological book *Pensées*. He said, "What else does this craving, and this helplessness, proclaim but that there was once in man a true happiness, of which all that now remains is the empty print and trace? This he tries in vain to fill with everything around him, seeking in things that are not there the help he cannot find in those that are, though none can help, since this infinite abyss can be filled only with an infinite and immutable object; in other words by God himself." We will look and search and crave—but until we come to the God who loves us we will remain unsatisfied.

To that end, we have assembled this collection of teaching, and we invite you to join us in life's greatest adventure—the adventure of knowing the Creator. We want to know and understand and share, not only the love of God but more important, the God of love. We want to explore His love and His Word—His role as our heavenly Father and what it means to live in relationship with Him. Ultimately, we want to see the God who loves us—for that is what the world really does need. Now and forever.

BILL CROWDER
Associate Bible Teacher,
RBC Ministries

ONE

GOD OUR FATHER

What It Means To Be His Child

I t's good to be emotionally stable, but it's more important to be in the hands of One who is greater than our problems. It's desirable to be born to non-abusive parents, but it's far better to be born into the family of God. It's beneficial to be employed in meaningful work, but it's eternally preferable to have a Provider who assures a security that exceeds all earthly benefits.

In the following pages, Kurt De Haan, who was the managing editor of *Our Daily Bread* until his death in 2003, describes the kind of relationship that when understood and entered into can give meaning, security, and perspective to every area of life. It's the kind of family tie that can give faith to the fearful, hope to the disillusioned, and love to those who are lonely and unprotected.

—MARTIN R. DE HAAN II

In Search Of The Perfect Father

Have you ever seen Scotland's Loch Ness monster? Caught a glimpse of the abominable snowman high in the Himalayas? Or spotted a perfect father anywhere on this planet?

No matter how thorough our search among the families on earth, and no matter how much we may love our own dad, we know all too well that every father has his flaws. It is also true that what we know about human fathers and what we have experienced as children will affect how eagerly or how apprehensively we approach the subject of this chapter—knowing and enjoying God as our Father.

> *"If you want to judge how well a person understands Christianity, find out how much he makes of the thought of . . . having God as his Father."*
>
> J. I. PACKER

For some of us, it will be a fairly comfortable process. If we had a great and loving dad, we will gladly embrace the biblical picture of God as the ultimate parent. If we didn't have that kind of father, we may have a longing to find the kind of father we never knew. Still others, though, may struggle with even thinking of God in terms of a father. If Dad was abusive, emotionally distant, or physically absent, it may take a deliberate, even painful effort to sort through the misconceptions and learn to cling to the life-changing truths of the right kind of fathering modeled by God.

Only Jesus has the perfect Father (Mt. 5:48), and He alone can help us to experience the close relationship with His Father that our hearts desire. Jesus told His disciples, "No one comes to the Father except through Me. If you had known Me, you would have known My Father also.... He who has seen Me has seen the Father" (Jn. 14:6-7,9). As the perfect Son of God, He revealed His Father perfectly, and He showed us how we could enjoy an incredible closeness with the Father.

No other relationship can be as fulfilling, for to know God as our Father is to know life as He intended it to be. Theologian J. I. Packer wrote, "If you want to judge how well a person understands Christianity, find out how much he makes of the thought of being God's child and having God as his Father. If this is not the thought that prompts and controls his worship and prayers and his whole outlook on life, it means that he does not understand Christianity very well" (*Knowing God*, InterVarsity Press, p.182).

Is that how you think and live each day? Do you enjoy a close relationship with the Father in heaven? Do you know how much He loves you and longs to care for you?

The purpose of this chapter is to help us to see the absolute perfection of our heavenly Father and to learn how to make the most of our relationship with Him.

What Does It Mean To Be God's Child?

Think back to a story you probably read as a child—*Cinderella*. In the popular English version that I remember, a poor peasant girl named Cinderella was living a slavelike existence with her ugly stepsisters and a tyrant of a stepmother (both are bad stereotypes!).

While the stepmother and stepsisters went to a ball at the king's palace, Cinderella had to stay home. But when she was magically transformed into a dazzling beauty, she set off for the palace in a pumpkin-turned-coach.

During the evening, the dashing young prince danced with Cinderella and fell in love. She had to rush home when the clock struck midnight, however, and accidentally left behind a glass slipper. The prince searched the kingdom to find the slipper's owner, and eventually he found that it fit Cinderella. He swept her off her feet, married her, and she became a royal princess, part of the royal family.

It's a great story. I think part of the reason so many of us like the tale is that we all like to imagine we too could be a child of a king—living like a princess or prince—with all the privileges that come with such a position. We're often frustrated by the daily drudgery or even mistreatment. We long to be treated as someone special.

The Bible describes something far better than any mythical tale of a peasant-turned-princess and something more real than imagining ourselves to be a child of a present-day world leader. The Bible states that common sinners can become children of the King of the universe.

In the pages that follow, we will examine six characteristics of what it means for a person to be a child of God.

FAMILY STATUS

When the fullness of the time had come, God sent forth His Son ... to redeem those who were under the law, that we might receive the adoption as sons. And because you are sons, God has sent forth the Spirit of His Son into your hearts, crying out, "Abba, Father!" Therefore you are no longer a slave but a son, and if a son, then an heir of God through Christ (GAL. 4:4-7).

Behold what manner of love the Father has bestowed on us, that we should be called children of God! (1 JN. 3:1).

Those are powerful words! Ordinary people like you and me can be called children of the Creator of the universe. That's worth thinking about.

Why do we need to become part of another family? An illustration from recent history will help us to realize the significance of this concept. The images are burned deeply into my memory— emaciated babies and young children sitting in cribs in a stark, ill-equipped Romanian orphanage.

It was soon after the fall of the ruthless leader Nicolae Ceausescu in 1989. Conditions were awful. Malnutrition, disease, and death were frequent visitors.

The good news was that when Ceausescu fell, the plight of the orphans became worldwide news—and compassionate people from all over the world rushed to help. Food, medicine, and money poured in. But the most dramatic effort of love was made by those who struggled through the red tape to adopt the orphans. Instead of being children of a ruthless government, they became children of parents who longed to love them and provide for them a life with hope and a future.

God has done something similar for us. We live in a world that is dominated by a heartless tyrant. The Bible describes Satan as "the ruler of this world" (Jn. 12:31; 16:11) and "the god of this age," who has blinded the minds of people so they do not believe in Christ (2 Cor. 4:4). Those who reject Christ are called children of the devil (Jn. 8:44).

This directly contradicts the concept of what has been called the universal fatherhood of God and the brotherhood of man. To say that God is the loving Father of all people and that no one will ever be judged as worthy of hell is a statement contrary to what Jesus and the Bible say about who qualifies to be a child of God. In 1 John 3:15 we learn that humanity can be divided into two categories: the children of God and the children of the devil. And Jesus told Paul that his mission in life would be to turn people "from darkness to light, and from the power of Satan to God" (Acts 26:18).

What has God done to bring us into His family?
The Bible uses two word pictures to explain this process. The first is what Jesus described as being "born again" (Jn. 3:3). The second is the concept we have already referred to—adoption (Rom. 8:15; Gal. 4:5; Eph. 1:5). Both analogies help us to understand the frequent biblical use of the expressions "sons of God" and "children of God."

Jesus said that a person is outside the family of God, spiritually condemned, unless he is spiritually reborn (Jn. 3:1-21). This rebirth is accomplished by God's Spirit when a person expresses personal faith in Jesus as his or her only hope of forgiveness of sin and life in heaven. The apostle John said that "as many as received [Jesus], to them He gave the right to become children of God, to those who believe in His name" (Jn. 1:12)

A person is outside the family of God unless he is spiritually reborn.

Adoption is the other key illustration used in the New Testament. In Romans 8:14-16, the apostle Paul wrote, "As many as are led by the Spirit of God, these are sons of God. For you did not receive the spirit of bondage again to fear, but you received the Spirit of adoption by whom we cry out, 'Abba, Father.' The Spirit Himself bears witness with our spirit that we are children of God."

Whereas the term *born again* may be said to refer primarily to the giving of new spiritual life and bringing a person into God's family, the term *adoption* highlights the new relationship with the Father and the new legal rights and privileges.

We are not only saved from an eternity in hell but we are also given a wonderful new status as children of God. Pastor and author Erwin Lutzer states, "Christ did not die on the cross just so our sins could be forgiven, though that itself would deserve our endless praise. Sin was a roadblock that God removed so He could achieve some lofty goals in our lives. Specifically, we have been appointed to be sons of God" (*You're Richer Than You Think*, SP Publications, p.47).

In Galatians 3:22–4:7, Paul highlighted many of the truths we have addressed so far:

- Until we become a child of God, we are spiritually dead, enslaved to sin (3:22-23; 4:3).
- One becomes a child of God by a personal expression of faith in Christ (3:26).
- God's Spirit gives us new life and makes us children of God (4:6).
- To be a child of God means both freedom from sin's bondage and incredible privileges now and forever as a spiritual heir (4:4-7).

How can being part of God's family change my life? That's what the rest of this chapter is all about. We will explore the biblical truths that we have free access to the Father in prayer, training in how to be

Christlike, help for every situation we face in life, a new perspective of hope for this life and eternity, and last but not least, we have responsibilities to fulfill to our Father and to our new brothers and sisters.

ACCESS THROUGH PRAYER

Through [Jesus] we both have access by one Spirit to the Father (EPH. 2:18).

When you pray, do not use vain repetitions as the heathen do. . . . For your Father knows the things you have need of before you ask Him. In this manner, therefore, pray: Our Father in heaven, hallowed be Your name (MT. 6:7-9).

Let us therefore come boldly to the throne of grace, that we may obtain mercy and find grace to help in time of need (HEB. 4:16).

The statements above would be seen as blasphemous if you believed that because God is perfect and separated from evil, He cannot be approached so casually, if at all, by people like you and me. Yet Jesus and His disciples have made it clear that we indeed can come to God in prayer because we are family through faith in Christ.

If I wanted to meet with a high-ranking federal government official, I would have to make an appointment—days or months in advance. But when I want to talk with my dad, what do I do? I simply drop by his home or pick up the phone and call him. Why? Because we're family.

My four children know they can come and talk to me anytime at all. No appointments are necessary. They don't have to put on their best clothes or even take a bath first. They don't have to use special language, kneel down, hold their hands a certain way, or follow an outline of what to say. Why? Because we're family.

We can call God "Abba." *Abba* is the Aramaic term that Jewish children use to address their fathers. (Aramaic is a language closely related to Hebrew and was commonly spoken during the time of Christ's ministry.) The English equivalent of *Abba* would be the terms *Daddy* or *Dear Father*. Although the term was originally derived from babytalk, by the time of Christ it was a word used by young and old alike to speak in an intimate way to their fathers.

The New Testament was written in Greek (the trade language of the wider Mediterranean world), so the word we usually find for "father" is *pater*. But because the common language of the day in Palestine was Aramaic, we have good reason to believe that when Jesus taught His disciples to pray, "Our Father in heaven, hallowed be Your name" (Mt. 6:9), He told them to use the term *Abba*.

In Romans 8:15, the apostle Paul said that because we are God's adopted children, we can cry out "Abba, Father" (this phrase is also used in Mark 14:36 and Galatians 4:6). Concerning this verse, Bible commentator F. F. Bruce writes that the use of *Abba* is significant because "Abba was not, and is not the term used by Jews when addressing God as their

Father. But the fact that the Aramaic word found its way into the worshiping vocabulary of the Gentile churches strongly suggests that it was used in this way by Jesus" (*The Epistle Of Paul To The Romans*, Eerdmans, p.166).

Why is this privilege so significant? The Old Testament emphasizes God's awesome holiness to such a degree that He does not seem approachable. The tabernacle and temple reinforced this idea by both structure and ritual. God's special presence was not something that everyone could enter—only the high priest and then only once a year.

In his book *What Jesus Said About Successful Living*, Haddon W. Robinson writes, "In the Old Testament, the Israelites did not individually address God as Father. As far as we know, Abraham, Joseph, Moses, David, or Daniel never fell to their knees in the solitude of their chambers and dared to address God that way. Yet in the New Testament, God is called Father at least 275 times, and that is how we are instructed to speak to Him. All that a good father wants to be to his children, Jesus told us, God will be to Christians who approach Him in prayer. We can pray as children" (Discovery House Publishers, p.190).

In the New Testament, we have a clear picture of the believer's privilege to call God "Father." It is central to the gospel message and to the way we are to live as Christ's followers. God's holiness and greatness is not diminished by this in the least because in Christ we have a mediator who satisfies

God's requirements for holiness and who makes us holy by His sacrifice for our sins (1 Tim. 2:5; Heb. 8:6; 9:15; 12:24). We can now come before Him with a God-sanctioned boldness (Eph. 3:12; Heb. 4:16; 10:19).

Isn't there a danger of taking prayer too lightly? There certainly is. As we embrace the refreshing truth that we have unhindered access to God through Jesus Christ, we must not forget that God is truly awesome. Haddon Robinson states, "The fact that we come to a throne should fill us with awe. But because it is a throne of grace, it's approachable . . . We can intimately and confidently talk with our Father" (*What Jesus Said About Successful Living*, p.191).

What is your prayer-life like? I don't know about you, but these truths from the Bible help me to see that heaven's door is always open to me as a member of God's family. The Father is eagerly anticipating my next visit, longing to hear my words of affection, to hear of my struggles, to hear my expressions of trust, and to hear the requests that show my realization that I depend on Him for everything in life. I hope you too are sensing the wonderful privilege and opportunity we have as God's children.

TRAINING IN GODLINESS

Whom the Lord loves He corrects, just as a father the son in whom he delights (PROV. 3:12).

We have had human fathers who corrected us, and we paid them respect. Shall we not much more readily be in subjection to the Father of spirits and live? For they indeed for a few days chastened us as seemed best to them, but He for our profit, that we may be partakers of His holiness (HEB. 12:9-10).

Training is a topic that most of us would rather not discuss. That's because we don't enjoy the pain that is necessary for learning and maturing. Training takes many forms. It may be physical: trying to get our body in shape by eating less and exercising more. It may be emotional and spiritual: learning how to depend on the Lord when tragedy strikes. Or it may take the form of suffering the consequences of sinful choices and experiencing the Lord's rebuke: learning "the hard way."

As children, we didn't enjoy the "lessons" our parents tried to teach us. Cleaning our rooms, helping with household chores, and doing our homework were generally not what we would have chosen to do with our time. And when we violated the rules, we didn't enjoy being sent to our room, getting spanked, being forced to do extra chores, or getting punished in some other way. At the time we received the discipline, we didn't have much appreciation for what we learned.

My father had a way of reminding his four sons that he didn't enjoy having to discipline us. Just before spanking one of us, he would say, "This is going to hurt me more than it will you." Many times, I'm sure, we had a hard time believing that. But now, as a father of four children myself, I understand what he meant. And it seems I spend quite a bit of time thinking through the type of discipline to use and the goal I want to achieve with my children. All of this has helped me to understand a little more of what it means for God to discipline us.

How does God train His children? As we have already illustrated, discipline can be either positive or negative. It can be training—instruction in how to live. Or it can take the form of correction—punishment for wrongdoing.

The author of Hebrews refers to both types of discipline. After a lengthy chapter in which he listed believers whose faith was severely tested by difficulties, persecution, and even martyrdom, he began chapter 12 by reminding his readers that we need to follow the examples of faithfulness of the past and to endure all difficulties as we follow Christ's example. Using athletic imagery, he told us to get in shape spiritually and not to allow anything to slow us down as we "run with endurance the race that is set before us" (v.1).

Then the writer pointed to Jesus Christ as the ultimate example to follow (vv.2-3). Hebrews 5:8 says this about Christ: "Though He was a Son, yet He learned obedience by the things which He suffered." That is not to say that Christ was in any way sinful. It does say, however, that through the suffering He endured, Christ experienced everything that the Father wanted Him to, and by that experience He earned the qualifications to be the Savior of the world. Jesus Himself learned the high cost of obedience to the Father.

If Jesus Christ had to undergo such training, how could we ever question why God allows us to undergo training of a similar nature?

Hebrews 12 also speaks of discipline that is corrective, that which is a result of our sin. Verse 6 states that the Lord "scourges every son whom He receives." God sometimes has to take drastic measures in dealing with His children.

The New Testament church in Corinth, for example, had several members who needed correction (1 Cor. 11:17-34). They had lost touch with the reason for observing the Lord's Supper, and some were even getting drunk! As a result of God's discipline, several were suffering physically and some even died because of their callous attitude.

Why should we be glad that God disciplines His children? It demonstrates His love. Hebrews 12:5 quotes Proverbs 3:12 and says that as a good human father corrects his children, God corrects those whom He loves.

Paul Dwight Moody, son of evangelist D. L. Moody (1837-1899), told how his dad reflected the love of the heavenly Father in discipline. The incident took place when Paul was 10 years old. His dad had told him to finish talking with a visiting friend and then go to bed. But, Paul wrote, "A little later he came into the room again and saw that I had not obeyed him. Speaking with that directness of which he was capable, he ordered me to bed at once. His brusque tone of voice was new to me, and I retreated, frightened and in tears. But before I had time to fall asleep, he was at my bedside. He explained that he had reprimanded me because I had disobeyed him, but this in no way indicated that he didn't love me. As he knelt to pray with me, I noticed that tears were falling down over his rugged, bearded face. . . . I'll never forget the scene. My father had unknowingly awakened within me the consciousness of the love of God."

What is the goal of discipline? The Father's goal is to make us more like Christ. He doesn't want to hurt us; He wants to better us. Hebrews 12:10-11 tells us that God wants us to be "partakers of His holiness" and to produce "the peaceable fruit of righteousness." And according to James 1:2-5, the "testing" of our faith "produces patience" with the goal of making us spiritually mature.

Pastor Jim Carpenter writes, "Your heavenly Father never makes a mistake in discipline. His timing is perfect, His motives are pure, and His methods are never destructive. They are always beneficial" (*Discipleship Journal*, Issue 51, p.52).

Do we believe it? Are we convinced that everything God allows to happen in our lives is training of one sort or another—with the goal of making us more like Christ? It's true. It is this truth that puts all of the good and bad in life in perspective. With a goal so grand and noble, nothing in life is too bad to endure. And if we are willing to accept that, our attitude then must be, "Lord, whatever it takes, make me like Your Son Jesus Christ."

HELP IN TIMES OF NEED

A father of the fatherless, a defender of widows, is God in His holy habitation (Ps. 68:5).

Do not worry, saying, "What shall we eat?" or "What shall we drink?" or "What shall we wear?"... For your heavenly Father knows that you need all these things (Mt. 6:31-32).

What man is there among you who, if his son asks for bread, will give him a stone? Or if he asks for a fish, will he give him a serpent? If you then, being evil, know how to give good gifts to your children, how much more will your Father who is in heaven give good things to those who ask Him! (Mt. 7:9-11).

As a dad, I was always eager to come to my children's aid. It may have been a skinned arm or leg that needed some cleaning up, a bandage, and most of all, a little sympathy. It may have been some help in trying to understand a tough homework assignment. It could have been help in handling a conflict with a fellow student or a neighbor. It could have been protecting them from a large, mean-looking dog that suddenly showed up in our front yard. Sometimes it was simply a hug when my children were feeling left out or lonely.

How do we know our Father in heaven will

help us in our times of need? What kind of Father would He be if He didn't? Jesus answered this question in Matthew 7. He said that it's unthinkable that a father would be so cruel that he would give a stone to a hungry child who asks for some bread or a snake to one who asks for fish (vv.9-10). Then He drew a comparison: If we, as imperfect and sinful as we are, know how to give what is good to our children, how much more will our absolutely perfect Father give good things to us (v.11).

In his commentary on this passage, William Hendriksen writes, "The heavenly Father will not disappoint His children. This, however, does not mean that He will always give them whatever they ask. It means that He will not give them anything that is bad for them. He will give 'good things' to those who ask Him" (*The Gospel Of Matthew*, Baker Book House, p.363).

The Bible assures us that we can cast all our cares on Him because He cares for us (1 Pet. 5:7). He knows our needs, and He knows how to meet those needs with wisdom and compassion.

The Old Testament prophet Isaiah provides us with an interesting picture of God's care for His spiritual children. During a difficult time when Israel was being defeated by her enemies and God seemed to be far away, the people said, "The Lord has forsaken me, and my Lord has forgotten me." But God answered, "Can a woman forget her nursing child, and not have compassion on the son of her womb? Surely they may forget, yet I will not forget you. See, I have inscribed you on the palms of My hands" (Isa. 49:15-16).

We too can be certain that the One who gave us spiritual birth will never abandon us nor fail us.

What kinds of help do we need? Here are some examples of the kind of help we need and Bible verses (look them up) that indicate how God will supply those needs.

- Receiving basic physical needs (Mt. 6:31-32).
- Having wisdom to know what to say in tough witnessing situations (Mt. 10:18-20).
- Knowing how to pray (Rom. 8:26).
- Dealing with suffering (Rom. 8:18-30).
- Coping with illness (2 Cor. 12:7-10; Jas. 5:16).
- Resisting temptation (Rom. 6:1-23; 8:12-17; 1 Cor. 10:13).
- Needing comfort (2 Cor. 1:3-7).
- Facing intense pressures (2 Cor. 1:8-11).
- Resisting Satan (Eph. 6:10-18; Jas. 4:7).
- Coping with trials (Jas. 1:5).
- Overcoming worry (1 Pet. 5:7).

How has God demonstrated His loving care in times past? As we read the Bible, we find many examples of God's help in times of need. He has shown that He is the eager provider and protector of His children. The nation of Israel, for example, experienced the love of the Father throughout its history. In thinking back to the time the Lord brought the people out of Egypt, Moses said, "The Lord your God carried you, as a father carries his son, all the way you went until you reached this place" (Dt. 1:31 NIV).

The Bible contains many other examples too numerous to mention here. People like Abraham, Isaac, Ishmael, Joseph, Ruth, Daniel, Esther, Paul, and John could testify to God's provision and protection.

How has God shown His loving care to you? The truths we have been talking about may mean little to you if you don't recognize that God wants to care for you too. If you are His child through faith in Christ, He's already done a lot for you, and He longs to do more.

The evidence of His care may come through the people He sends into your life to meet your needs and encourage you. It may come through a deep peace in your heart as you express your trust in Him and cast all your cares on Him (1 Pet. 5:7). It may come through the supply of your physical needs or the grace and strength to endure great difficulty (2 Cor. 12:9; Phil. 4:11). You can be sure that your Father cares for you.

ETERNAL HOPE

[I pray] that the God of our Lord Jesus Christ, the Father of glory, may give to you the spirit of wisdom and revelation. . . ; that you may know what is the hope of His calling, what are the riches of the glory of His inheritance in the saints (EPH. 1:17-18).

We know that all things work together for good to

those who love God . . . . If God is for us, who can be against us? (ROM. 8:28,31).

In My Father's house are many mansions; if it were not so, I would have told you. I go to prepare a place for you. And if I go and prepare a place for you, I will come again and receive you to Myself (JN. 14:2-3).

Hope is what keeps you and me alive. People who lose hope of some sort or another usually become an enemy of society or a drain upon it. People without some glimmer of hope lash out or drop out. They become suicidal—by their reckless behavior in search of a temporary thrill or by blatant acts of despair that lead them to try to end it all by jumping, overdosing, or shooting.

What hope keeps people going from day to day? The hope of a paycheck? The thought of what they're going to do tomorrow or on the weekend? A vacation? A six-pack in the refrigerator? A warm relationship? A promotion? A high school diploma? A college degree? A new baby? A new house? Retirement? Recognition and reward from family, co-workers, friends, fellow churchgoers? Religion and the thought of eventual reward from God?

At the core of all the religions of the world is a quest for hope—something that makes sense of the apparent chaos and injustices of life. Men and women long to know why they exist, where they are going, and what makes it all worthwhile. Tragically, so many people are clinging to false hope.

The apostle Paul, when speaking to a group of

philosophers in first-century Athens, tried to help them see the futility of their thinking and to see that the only true hope is in Jesus Christ (Acts 17:16-34). Paul had observed idol after idol in the city (v.16)— idols that represented false hope. So he pointed to the Creator who could be known (v.27). There is hope in this life and beyond the grave (v.31). That hope is centered in knowing God as He has revealed Himself through His Son Jesus Christ and in trusting Him for forgiveness of sin.

In a letter to the believers in Ephesus, Paul described their condition before they had learned about Christ and put their trust in Him. He said, "At that time you were without Christ, . . . having no hope and without God in the world" (Eph. 2:12).

Why do we have reason to hope? We are part of a family that has a loving heavenly Father and a Son who has opened the door to hope.

Paul also told the Ephesians he was praying that they would realize just how great the hope of believers is through Christ (1:17-18). He prayed that they would get to know God the Father better and realize all that He offers His children. Let's examine a few of the reasons we have for hope in this life and beyond.

What is our basis for hope?

- We have been given spiritual life and are freed from Satan's death-grip (Eph. 2:1-7).
- We have been given the inner presence of the Holy Spirit, who confirms that we are God's children (Rom. 8:16) and guarantees

that our adoption is forever (Eph. 1:13-14).

- We have God's power enabling us to live for Him (2 Cor. 12:9; Eph. 1:19).
- We have assurance that nothing can separate us from God's love (Rom. 8:35-39).
- We have confidence that all the events of life—good and bad—have a purpose (Rom. 8:28) and that God is in control (vv.29-39).
- We have the promise that we can be forgiven of sin and restored to a close relationship with the Father if we confess (1 Jn. 1:5-10).
- We have the guarantee of our Father's help as we live for Him (see section "Help in Times of Need" p.27).
- We have a Father who hears and answers prayer (see section "Access Through Prayer" p.19).
- We have the encouragement that comes from belonging to a family where each is spiritually gifted for the good of others (Rom. 12:1-8; Eph. 4:1-16; Heb. 10:25).
- We have the promise of an abundant, meaningful life (Jn. 10:10).
- We have God's Word to guide us and equip us for every task (2 Tim. 3:16-17).

What is our hope for eternity?

- We look forward to a coming resurrection (Acts 24:15; 1 Cor. 15).
- We have a heavenly home waiting for us, specially prepared by Christ (Jn. 14:1-6).
- We will be with Christ Himself (1 Jn. 3:2;

2 Cor. 5:6-9; Rev. 21–22).

- We will be like Christ (1 Jn. 3:2)—having a new body that is free from the ravages of sin (2 Cor. 5:1-5).
- We will be reunited with our believing loved ones (1 Th. 4:13-18).
- We will receive an inheritance far beyond our greatest dreams (Eph. 1:11,14,18; Col. 1:12; 1 Pet. 1:3-4).
- Our service for Christ and the sacrifices we made for Him will be richly rewarded (1 Cor. 3:9-15; 9:16-27; Col. 3:24).
- We will experience relief from every kind of sorrow we knew on earth (Rev. 21:4).

Do you have hope? As we have just seen, we have plenty of reasons to be hopeful about this life and the life to come. It's easy to become preoccupied with troubles that confront us daily. Some of those difficulties may appear insurmountable. That's all the more reason we should purposefully and regularly set aside time to review these reasons for hope. No matter how hopeless life may seem at the moment, we have reason for hope on earth because we have a Father in heaven.

RESPONSIBILITIES TO FULFILL

As obedient children, . . . be holy in all your conduct, because it is written, "Be holy, for I am holy." And if you call on the Father, who without partiality judges accord-

ing to each one's work, conduct yourselves throughout the time of your stay here in fear (1 PET. 1:14-17).

You shall be perfect, just as your Father in heaven is perfect (MT. 5:48).

In this the children of God and the children of the devil are manifest: Whoever does not practice righteousness is not of God, nor is he who does not love his brother (1 JN. 3:10).

To be God's child is great, and it has many benefits that we can feel thrilled to be able to enjoy. We've spent the major part of this chapter detailing many of those privileges. But there's another important and inescapable side to this relationship: God's children have responsibilities to fulfill.

What do we expect from our own children? It's heartbreaking to listen to an elderly parent talk about a son or daughter who finished school, got a job, moved out of the house, and hardly ever stops by to visit or even call Mom and Dad. We grieve with the parent of a rebellious 17-year-old who seems intent on playing the party scene and turning his back on God and the church. And we're sympathetic with the parents of a preschooler who runs away in a store when they say, "Come back here!"

I don't know how it was around your house, but when I was growing up one thing was clear: Being a child involved giving as well as taking. In spite of my stubborn tendency to do otherwise, I was expected to treat my parents with proper respect, to trust their judgment, to listen to them attentively, to do what they said to do (such as chores), and to treat my brothers well. I also learned that doing all those things was a lot more enjoyable if I was aware of my parents' love and their desire to help me, not hurt me.

Now that I am deep into parenthood, I have the perspective from the other side. And I realize how much it must have pleased my parents when I treated them right (which I didn't always do). And I also realize that the response I desire most from my children is not just obedience but an expression of love.

What does God want from us? The New Testament contains many exhortations to exhibit the right conduct or develop the proper attitudes. And very often those commands are within the context of our relationship with God our Father and the family of believers. Let's look at several examples.

The Father desires our love most of all. What did Jesus say when a legal expert asked Him, "Which is the greatest commandment in the Law?" (Mt. 22:36 NIV). Jesus replied, "'Love the Lord your God with all your heart and with all your soul and with all your mind.' This is the first and greatest commandment" (vv.37-38).

It's one thing to go through the motions of obeying out of duty, but it's quite another to serve God out of genuine devotion, telling Him often that we love Him. Have you told your heavenly Father recently that you love Him?

What this means to our heavenly Father was

illustrated to me by one of my daughters when she was two years old. She had learned the mechanics of saying, "I love you," by mimicking Mom and Dad, but on one occasion her words took on special meaning. One evening while we were playing together, she ran to me, put her little arms around my neck, and said, "I love you, Daddy!" That moment was precious to me. Her words went straight to my heart because they were sincere, unrehearsed, and pure.

As we think about who our heavenly Father is, how much He loves us, and all He does for us, we too will find ourselves running to Him in prayer and saying, "I love You, Father!"

The Father deserves honor. At the end of the Old Testament, the Lord asked the leaders of His chosen people some soul-searching questions: "A son honors his father, and a servant his master. If then I am the Father, where is My honor? And if I am a Master, where is My reverence?" (Mal. 1:6).

We learned earlier of the tremendous privilege we have to call the almighty Creator by the intimate term *Abba*. But we must never forget who He is— the sovereign Lord of all that exists.

To honor the Father also means to recognize that He is the provider of all that we have and enjoy. We are to be "always giving thanks to God the Father for everything" (Eph. 5:20 NIV).

The Father wants us to imitate Him. Erwin Lutzer writes, "If a man says, 'My father is Mr. Jones,' you look at his face to see if you can see any resemblance to his father. So when a believer says, 'I am a son of God,' we should expect that his life will have at least some trace of the character of God" (*You're Richer Than You Think*, Victor Books, p.55).

The apostle Paul wrote, "Be imitators of God as dear children. And walk in love, as Christ also has loved us and given Himself for us" (Eph. 5:1-2). We are imitators of God also when we are merciful as He is merciful (Lk. 6:36).

The family resemblance is seen in our clean break from a godless way of life. We are to be clearly different from people who are not members of God's family. In 1 John we read, "This is how we know who the children of God are and who the children of the devil are: Anyone who does not do what is right is not a child of God" (3:10 NIV).

Although we are "born again" by faith (Jn. 3:3,16), we demonstrate the reality of that faith by acts of obedience to God. James said, "Faith by itself, if it does not have works, is dead" (2:17). Jesus taught, "Whoever does the will of My Father in heaven is My brother and sister and mother" (Mt. 12:50). He also said, "Not everyone who says to Me, 'Lord, Lord,' shall enter the kingdom of heaven, but he who does the will of My Father in heaven" (7:21).

So our pattern of behavior, whether obedience or disobedience, reveals to whose family we belong.

What responsibilities do we have to other members of the family? Romans 12:5 reminds us that we are closely linked to other children of God. We may not recognize it or consistently act like it, but all who come to God through faith in Christ are members of the same family: "We, being many, are one body in Christ, and individually members of one another."

It must hurt the Father to see His children at odds with each other. It hurts me deeply when my children fight and I hear a comment like, "She hates me!" It is painful to see them not wanting to help each other. How much more it must make our Father's heart ache to see the kind of "warfare" that goes on among believers.

As members of a spiritual family, we must put aside our self-centeredness and look out for the interests of one another. Our responsibilities include the following:

- We are to love one another. The obligation we have to other children of God, just as in our relationship with God, is love (Rom. 13:8; 1 Cor. 13; 1 Th. 3:12; 4:9; 1 Pet. 3:8; 4:8; 1 Jn. 3:11,23; 4:7,11-12).
- We are to honor one another through service (Rom. 12:10; Gal. 5:13; 1 Pet. 4:10).
- We are to be generous and hospitable (Rom. 12:13; 1 Pet. 4:9).
- We are to do all we can to build up one another spiritually, not tear each other down (Rom. 14:13).
- We are to teach each other (Rom. 15:14).
- We are to be truthful (Eph. 4:25; Col. 3:9).
- We are to be kind and forgiving (Eph. 4:32; Col. 3:13).
- We are to comfort one another in times of need (1 Th. 5:11).

- We are to challenge each other to live holy lives (Heb. 3:13; 10:24-25).
- We are to pray for one another (Jas. 5:16).

Are we fulfilling our responsibilities joyfully? We've listed many obligations that we have to our heavenly Father and to our brothers and sisters in Christ. As we read such a list, we may tend to feel like a child who just received a list of chores to do on Saturday morning before he can play with his friends.

That's why we need to remind ourselves continually of what will motivate us to do all these things with the right attitude—a recognition that we are family. We are part of a spiritual family headed by a loving Father who, out of love for us, has gone to great lengths, even sacrificing His own Son Jesus Christ, to bring us into His family.

As we think of all He has done for us and how much He loves us, our hearts and lives cannot help but respond with the kind of loving words and actions that will please Him and create a closer family among those who also have been adopted by Him.

Are You A Member Of The Family?

It's the most important issue of life: Can you say that God is your Father? Have you become a child of God by declaring your personal faith in Jesus as Savior? Your answer determines whether all the joys of knowing God as Father now and throughout eternity will be yours.

Perhaps you've read this chapter with an uneasy feeling that you are not a member of the family. Now is a good time to settle the issue.

The Father longs to adopt you, and the procedure is simple. Come to Him in childlike faith, accepting His offer of forgiveness from your sins, which have kept you out of the family. Jesus lived, died, and rose from the grave to show you the Father's love and to make it possible to for you to become a member of God's family.

The Father is waiting to hear from you. He does not expect flowery words, just a simple expression of childlike faith. Tell Him that you believe Jesus died to pay the penalty for your sins. Accept His gift of forgiveness (Rom. 6:23) and the invitation to be part of His family forever.

If you truly believe in Jesus and what He did for you, welcome to the family!

TWO

HOW
HAS GOD
LOVED US?

These words come from the pen of a Jewish prophet named Malachi. As the last spokesman of the Old Testament, he raised a troubling question. How can we take comfort in the love of God if we don't feel loved? What if circumstances seem to say that God is ignoring us, that He has abandoned us to our own pain, and that He is deliberately withholding from us what He could so easily grant?

Malachi, a messenger to God's "chosen people," assures us that we are not the first to ask such questions. He gives us a chance to see why the love of God is one of the most misunderstood truths of the Bible.

—MARTIN R. DE HAAN II

What Do You Believe About The Love Of God?

- "I think He loves us unconditionally, whether we love Him or not."
- "I believe God loves us. But that doesn't mean I'm religious. The way I see it, if God loves us, what do we have to worry about?"
- "I want to believe God loves us. But that might be reading too much human emotion into Him."
- "I used to believe in a God of love. But some things have happened to me that I really don't want to talk about."
- "I think God loves us, but it's probably a different kind of love than we show for one another. I think He loves us in ways that we might not even recognize as love."
- "I believe God loves me. But I often have a hard time reconciling that with the way I'm feeling about myself."

THE QUESTION HAS A HISTORY

Conflicting opinions about the love of God are more than a symptom of our times. Confusion about whether God cares about us can be traced all the way back to the closing days of the Old Testament. Even then, some of the most religious people in the world were wondering how they could believe in a God who said He loved them while acting as though He didn't. In about 450 BC, Malachi, the last of the Old Testament prophets, said to the people of Jerusalem, " 'I have loved you,' says the Lord. But you ask, 'How have You loved us?' " (Mal. 1:2 NIV).

THERE WERE OTHER QUESTIONS

The book of Malachi has come down to us as a two-way conversation between God and His "chosen nation." Eighteen times Malachi asked questions on behalf of God. Ten times he asked questions on behalf of his Jewish countrymen. Through the pen of Malachi, Israel answered God's questions with more of their own:

* How have You loved us? (1:2).
* How have we shown contempt for You? (1:6).
* How can You say we've defiled You? (1:7).
* Why don't You answer our prayers? (2:13-14).
* How have we wearied You? (2:17).
* Where is Your sense of fairness? (2:17).
* How do You expect us to return to You? (3:7).
* How have we robbed You? (3:8).
* What have we said against You? (3:13).
* What did we gain by serving You? (3:14).

PUT THESE QUESTIONS IN ANOTHER CONTEXT

To see how amazing these questions are, put them in the mouth of a wife who after 50 years of marriage still isn't convinced that her husband loves her. Imagine overhearing one side of a telephone conversation in which a 75-year-old woman says to her husband, "How can you say you have loved me? Is this the way a man loves his wife, by saying she has had contempt for him? How have I hurt you? You don't even pay attention to me anymore. I talk, but you don't listen. Then you say I'm the one who wore you down. Where is your sense of decency? How, after all that has gone on between us, could you expect me to have the affection I used to have for you? You say you love me, yet in the very same breath you accuse me of ruining your name and reputation. You call this love? I don't think so. I don't know what I've gained by living for these 50 years locked to the chains of your demands."

Israel, at the end of her Old Testament history, was talking like this woman. She had been married to Yahweh for 1,000 years. Yet when told of God's love, she acted like she hadn't seen it.

Modern Jewish humor reflects the irony of a chosen people who have often felt unloved by God: "An old Jew prayed fervently in the synagogue, 'Lord, 4,000 years ago, on the slopes of Mount Sinai, You chose the Jews as a people peculiar to You, a holy people, a nation of priests, to bear the yoke of Your holy Law and to serve as witness to all the world. Lord, I am deeply sensible of the honor, but Lord, enough is enough. Surely it is time You chose somebody else" (*Isaac Asimov's Treasury Of Humor*).

Gentiles have been known to pray a similar

prayer: "Lord, if this is what it means to be loved by You, then please love someone else for a while."

Such prayers reflect our need for a clearer sense of what it means to be loved by God.

A Simple Way Of Looking At A Complex Subject

The Bible says that God is love and that the whole of His law can be reduced to the principle of doing for others as we would want them to do for us (Mt. 22:37-39; Gal. 5:14). The Scriptures make it just as apparent, however, that there is profound complexity behind this simple principle.

Before taking a closer look at the questions and answers of Malachi, let's use a visual image to illustrate the simplicity and complexity of our subject. As a prism separates a simple shaft of light into a spectrum of colors, so the Scriptures separate the love of God into different shades of meaning.

GOD LOVES IN DIFFERENT WAYS

While the Bible says that God is love, it also shows us that He loves in different ways, in different degrees, and with different results. Until we carefully work through the principles and specific examples of His love, it can seem very confusing. For example, the Bible tells us that God loves impartially and without prejudice, but He also chose the nation of Israel to be the special object of His love. He loves in time, and He loves in eternity. Sometimes His love is tough, and sometimes it is tender. He loves some as they choose their way to heaven and others as they choose their way to hell. To sort out such seemingly conflicting evidence, it is important for us to see some of the different ways God loves us.

GOD LOVES UNCONDITIONALLY

The Bible makes it clear that in so many ways, God loves us because of who He is rather than because of who we are. He offers to be our God not because we are lovable but because He is loving. He offers to care for us not because of our performance, our goodness, or even because of our effort or good intentions. He loves us because that's the kind of God He is.

This is the kind of unconditional love God showed the nation of Israel when He made them His "chosen people." He did not choose Abraham's family because they were deserving (Dt. 7:7; 9:4-6). He didn't choose them because of their numbers or because of their goodness. He chose them because it was within His right and power to use Abraham's descendants to tell the story of His love.

Many years later, a son of Israel taught His disciples to show one another the kind of unconditional love that God had shown them. This Teacher said:

*You have heard that it was said, "You shall love
your neighbor and hate your enemy." But I say to
you, love your enemies, bless those who curse you,
do good to those who hate you, and pray for those
who spitefully use you and persecute you, that you
may be sons of your Father in heaven; for He makes
His sun rise on the evil and on the good, and sends
rain on the just and on the unjust. For if you love
those who love you, what reward have you? Do not
even the tax collectors do the same?* (MT. 5:43-46).

We'll see more evidence of God's unilateral willingness to love us in pages 62-70 of this chapter.
There we will see how God makes it possible for us
to say that nothing can separate us from the love of
God (Rom. 8:35-39). But for now it's important to
understand that there is both an unconditional side
to God's love as well as a conditional side.

GOD LOVES CONDITIONALLY

Jesus reflected this side of God's love when He said
to His disciples, "The Father Himself loves you,
because you have loved Me, and have believed that
I came forth from God" (Jn. 16:27). While caring for
everyone, God has a special "family love" for those
who believe in His Son. This love is a special love
that goes beyond His affection for the whole world.

Years later, the apostle Paul wrote, "God loves a
cheerful giver" (2 Cor. 9:7). Again, while God cares
about the well-being of self-centered people, we
must conclude that in some affectional ways He

loves (or values) a generous person more than a tightfisted one.

If the different ways God loves are not considered, we might make the mistake of thinking that because He has been kind to us, He has unconditionally accepted us as His children. Or we might forget that His children can still act in ways that deepen His affections or arouse His anger.

God is a Person whose love must be understood in the richness and fullness of His whole personality. He is love. But He is not only love. He loves according to the counsel of His wisdom, His goodness, and His eternality. His love is not blind or indulgent or shortsighted. His love is tough, it's tender, it's on His terms rather than ours, and it's for the sake of His glory rather than our desires.

How Has God Loved Us?

Keeping in mind that God loves us in a spectrum of ways, let's take a closer look at Malachi's answer to the question, "How has God loved us?"

God has loved us in ways we tend to overlook *(Mal. 1:2-4).* God reminded the people of Jerusalem of something as obvious as their own national existence. After 70 years of exile in Babylon, they were back in their mother city. Even though they were not satisfied with the conditions of their life, God had not forgotten them. He had given them favor with the

Persian conquerors of Babylon. He had brought them back to the homeland they loved.

The same could not be said for their cousins, the Edomites. While the descendants of Jacob had been given a land with cities they hadn't built, homes they hadn't filled, wells they hadn't dug, and vineyards and olive groves they hadn't planted (Dt. 6:10-12), the descendants of Jacob's twin brother Esau had the opposite experience. God put the Edomites under a national curse. He called attention to their pride and said that even if they built their homes in mountain fortresses, He would make their homes a wasteland (Mal. 1:4). Esau's descendants would try to get up, but God would knock them down.

To this day, the obvious physical contrast between the "mountain of Jacob" and the "mountain of Esau" is apparent. Even though the descendants of Esau built strongholds high in the cliffs of Sela (in Petra, which is 50 miles south of the Dead Sea), God made their cliff dwellings desolate—a striking evidence of His judgment (see Obad. 8-18).

The Lord's choice of Jacob over his twin brother Esau was not an expression of favoritism. God didn't indulge Israel like a spoiled child or give His people immunity from the consequences of their sins. With Israel's increased privilege came increased responsibility. No other nation would end up being known as the "people of the Holocaust."

God chose Israel not only to show the world the enviable condition of those who trust Him but also to show the desolation that comes to those who refuse His offer of love.

God's chosen people ended up asking, "How have You loved us?" Their question is a reminder that sometimes our need is not to have more knowledge but to pray that we don't miss the obvious.

Isaac Asimov tells a tongue-in-cheek account of Sir Arthur Conan Doyle, author of the famous Sherlock Holmes stories. He says that Doyle once hailed a cab in Paris, threw his handbag inside, and climbed in after it. But before he could say a word, the driver said, "Where to, Mr. Conan Doyle?" "You recognize me?" said the author in surprise. "Not really. I've never seen a picture of you." "Then how do you know I am Conan Doyle?" "Well," said the driver, "I had read in the newspapers that you were on vacation in the south of France. I noticed you getting off a train that came from Marseille. I see you have the kind of tan that bespeaks a week or more in the sun. From the inkspot on your right middle finger, I deduce that you are a writer. You have the keen look of a medical man, and the cut of clothes of an Englishman. Putting it all together, I felt you must surely be Conan Doyle, the creator of the great detective, Sherlock Holmes." Conan Doyle burst out, "But you are yourself the equal of Sherlock Holmes since you recognized me from all these small observations." "There is," said the driver, "one additional fact. Your name is lettered on your handbag."

In the details of life, we can miss the obvious signature of love. In time, Israel forgot how loving God had been in making them His chosen people and the apple of His eye. So we too can forget that our very existence reflects the many obvious ways God has loved us.

God has loved us enough to expose our contempt for Him (*Mal.* 1:6-8). In the days of Malachi, the quality of life was declining in Jerusalem. Marriages were in trouble (2:14-16). Crime was a problem (3:5). Parent-child relationships were deteriorating (4:6). Spiritual leaders lacked integrity (2:7-9). People needed encouragement and words of comfort.

Malachi did comfort them. But he also showed them that while the love of God is wonderful, it is not necessarily safe. God loves us enough to make an issue of our sin. He loves us enough to show us that many of our personal and social problems are the result of our own contempt for God.

Malachi was direct. He seemed willing to make cases of bad self-esteem worse. Rather than choosing the words that would help troubled people feel better about themselves, he seemed intent on creating feelings of guilt and regret.

Shouldn't an understanding of Israel's troubled times have prompted a man of God to offer words of encouragement and hope? The people of Israel must have longed for a soothing voice from heaven to calm their fearful hearts and to inspire courage in the face of profound spiritual disappointment.

But Malachi's love was a tough love. He cared enough to warn those who were arousing the patient anger of God. He exposed the hearts of those who thought they could fulfill their obligations to God by offering that which cost them nothing. He confronted the priests who were willing to accept offerings of the crippled and blind animals of Israel's flocks (Mal. 1:8).

That such sacrifices were not acceptable to God appears to have been a surprise to Malachi's countrymen. Sacrificing defective animals seemed to meet the needs of both religion and business. It cleansed the flocks of bad stock while still providing something to burn on the altar. They could give something to God without depriving their families or businesses in the process.

The prophet pointed out, however, that these worthless sacrifices were not about meat. They were about hearts. A blind ram offered as a sin sacrifice reflected the spiritual blindness of the offerer. A crippled animal indicated an owner's twisted walk. These imperfect sacrifices were about people who, because they didn't fear God, were also more likely to divorce their partners, ignore their children, embezzle money, or neglect a neighbor's need.

Israel didn't see it that way. When confronted with their contempt for God, they acted perplexed. "In what way have we despised Your name? . . . In what way have we defiled You?" (1:6-7).

What Israel had forgotten is that we cannot treat God as One who will take just anything we give Him. He is a jealous God who asks for first place in our hearts. Such loyalty has parallels. A wife who walks into a restaurant and finds her husband showing affection for another woman isn't apt to be satisfied to be just one of his partners. Neither is God satisfied to be just one of our loves.

When any two relationships compete with each other, one must lose. Jesus said, "No one can serve two masters; for either he will hate the one and love the other, or else he will be loyal to the one and despise the other" (Mt. 6:24).

Instinctively, we want it to be different. We want to believe that we can serve more than one at a time. We want to believe that we can juggle our way through life keeping all the balls in the air and all the plates spinning. But God loves us enough to show that we cannot have it all. There is a trade-off for every choice. It's impossible to add without subtracting. Everything we add to our lives occupies its own place in space and time.

God loves us enough to confront our lack of respect for Him. He is not threatened by our anger or veiled contempt. He would rather have us confront the truth about ourselves than to go on thinking that we are doing better than we really are.

God has loved us enough to give us our freedom (*Mal.* 3:16–4:2). Malachi's countrymen responded in a variety of ways. Some feared God. Others didn't. In the process, God loved them enough to let them choose their own way. He cared for them enough to give them freedom to decide their own destiny. Some chose the path of spiritual safety. Some shook off the prophet's message and brought great loss to themselves, their families, and the reputation of their God.

It's often assumed that if God loves us, He is the one entity in life we don't have to worry about. In every generation, otherwise intelligent people lose their sense of reason when it comes to thinking about the love of God. They reason that if God loves us, He will be the Good Shepherd who loves us in spite of our actions toward Him. Bad things may happen for other reasons, they admit. But they cannot imagine that a loving God would ever let anything terrible happen as a result of what we believe or don't believe about Him.

But the last prophet of the Old Testament is like the last prophet of the New Testament. Both shake their readers out of romantic notions about the love of God. Both Malachi in the Old Testament and John in the New Testament book of Revelation reveal a God who loves us enough to allow for a freedom that is as dangerous as it is wonderful. Both speak of God's love for those who fear Him and the inevitable fiery judgment of those who don't.

While we might find it impossible to understand how God could allow anyone to choose the hell described by Jesus in His Sermon on the Mount (Mt. 5:22,29-30; 7:13-14), consider the alternative. The alternative to choice is no choice. To have no choice is to be less than human and to cease to exist in the likeness of God.

Choice is a part of the high calling given to us by God in His love. Accountability for our own decisions is part of what it means to be made in the image and likeness of God. With that capacity comes freedom unlike anything known either by the animal world below or the angelic world above. It is a freedom for enormous gain or loss.

Malachi reveals that God loves us enough to give us freedom of choice and also enough to take our decisions seriously. He cares when we make a worthless sacrifice to fulfill ritual obligations (Mal. 1:6-14). He sees us when we break our promises to one another (Mal. 2:11-16). He knows when we try to protect our financial interests by withholding from Him the faith He's asked for (Mal. 3:8-11). He cares when we fear Him, and He cares when we don't (Mal. 3:16—4:3).

God has shown special love to some for the sake of all *(Mal. 1:11; Rom. 11:11-14)*. God's purpose was never to make Israel the sole focus of His love. He had in view those Egyptians who would attach themselves to Hebrew friends when Israel was delivered from the Pharaoh. He had in mind Ruth the Moabite, who would say to a Jewish mother-in-law, "Your people shall be my people, and your God, my God" (Ruth 1:16). He had in mind the queen of Sheba, who would later travel a long way to see the extent of Solomon's riches and to learn the secret of his wisdom (1 Ki. 1:10-13).

These Gentiles were a partial fulfillment of the Lord's original intent to bless all the nations of the earth through the descendants of Abraham (Gen. 12:3). By choosing to make an example of Israel, the Lord gave everyone else reason to want what Israel had and to ask questions about her God.

At the end of Old Testament history, the Lord

used this same tactic on Israel. When Malachi wrote to Jerusalem in 450 BC, he called attention to the fact that God could be more pleased with the Gentiles than with Israel (1:11).

It's not too difficult to see how God could appeal to our envy. Many of us can see ourselves in the little child who discards his toys and treats them roughly until he sees another child pick them up and play with them. Many of us who are husbands know what it is to take our wife for granted until we see another man flirt with her.

God knows the feelings of envy that can be stirred up when we see someone else pick up the treasure of opportunity we have thrown away. Yet the Lord isn't just playing mind games with us. He is serious when He warns us that if we don't respond to His love, He will find someone else who will wholeheartedly embrace Him.

Notice what the apostle Paul said in Romans 11:11-14 about this issue:

> *I say then, have [the Jews] stumbled that they should fall? Certainly not! But through their fall, to provoke them to jealousy, salvation has come to the Gentiles. Now if their fall is riches for the world, and their failure riches for the Gentiles, how much more their fullness! For I speak to you Gentiles; inasmuch as I am an apostle to the Gentiles, I magnify my ministry, if by any means I may provoke to jealousy those who are my flesh and save some of them.*

By electing some to be the special objects of His grace, God is giving everyone reason to be envious of His love. Sometimes He uses Jews to make Gentiles envious. Sometimes he uses Gentiles to make Jews jealous. He loves us enough to appeal to our own nature to turn our hearts toward Him.

God has loved us enough to care how we treat one another (Mal. 2:14-17; 4:5-6). People who reject the love of God are likely to reject one another. Those who fail to find their inner security and significance in the Lord are apt to be driven by the kind of fears that causes them to be dangerous to others. Spiritually empty people tend to develop short-sighted strategies of self-protection. In a blind rush to protect their own interests, husbands reject their wives, parents ignore their children, and children despise their parents.

These are the social conditions reflected in the prophecy of Malachi. As the last prophet of the Old Testament, he reminded Israel that God hated the willful ways men were divorcing their wives. And in the last verse of that last prophecy, Malachi referred to broken parent-child relationships that had also resulted from Israel's spiritual failure.

Family conflict has been around for a long time. Most of it occurs when one or more members of a family lose a healthy sense of the fear and love of God. The husband and father who leaves his family to pursue another woman is often indulging a weak fear that he is not man enough to deal with the wife who knows his faults. Children who go silent or who lash out angrily also feel caught between contrary forces. Because they have not yet learned to find their security in God, they struggle with fears of being rejected by parents or friends.

Outwardly, we point our finger at one another. Instinctively, we raise issues of fairness and justice. We even turn against God Himself in our anger (Mal. 2:17). But behind the tough exterior are frightened people trying to scramble to protect their own interests. Behind the anger is usually wounded pride and a fearful heart.

Recognizing the fear behind the anger helps us to see what happens when individuals of any age or circumstance refuse to accept the security of the God who loves them.

Rejecting the security of the love of God results in rejecting one another to protect ourselves.

Rejecting or resisting the love of God puts all of us in a position to reject others, to protect ourselves from further pain. We may become emotionally detached, irritable, angry, demanding, or morally unprincipled. There are many self-destructive strategies for trying to protect ourselves from the painful rejection of others. But the underlying principle is always the same. Damaged people who are not rescued and controlled by the love of God try to avoid further pain and rejection by taking their safety into their own hands. The results are never good. Our efforts to protect ourselves from further rejection turn into more thoughts and feelings that take on a tormented life of their own.

These are the problems addressed by both secular and spiritual counselors. They plague religious as well as secular victims. When analyzed by themselves, they seem to be understandable results of understandable human dynamics.

As M. Scott Peck points out in *The Road Less Traveled*, hurt people tend to be marked by:

- avoidance of pain (indulgence),
- avoidance of responsibility (projection of blame),
- avoidance of reality/truth (flight from reality),
- avoidance of change (failure to balance).

Peck goes on to show how secular insight helps hurt people learn to (1) defer gratification, (2) accept responsibility for their own choices, (3) commit themselves to reality (rather than running from it), and (4) learn to balance their expectations of ever-changing circumstances.

Secular insight, however, leaves some important questions unanswered. As helpful as it is, it offers no real answers to the questions: Who am I? What is my real problem? How should I live? Who says I've got the ability to be what I should be?

It is in answering these questions that the Bible offers so much help in coming to terms with the problems of rejection and lost love. It is in answering these questions that the Bible goes on to show us how to rediscover the security and grace that we have rejected but now so desperately need.

The love of God that Malachi talked about did not end with the last of the Old Testament prophets. With the coming of night, a new dawn would follow.

Beyond Malachi

Today we see what the Jews of Malachi's day could not see. With the benefit of looking back 2,400 years, we can see how God was getting ready to make His name great among the Gentiles (Mal. 1:11). From a New Testament perspective, we can see how God would use Israel's rejection of His love as an occasion to offer Himself to the whole world. Through Israel's failure to appreciate His love, God would show it to people of all nations.

A NEW UNDERSTANDING

The New Testament has given us a new way to hear God when He says, "I have loved you." When we are inclined to answer back, "How have You loved us?" we have different information to deal with.

What the Old Testament Jews could not see was how far God would go to show His love for us. What they could not see is how emotionally, spiritually, and physically involved God would become to deal with the heartbreaking problem of our sin.

Today we can read several different New Testament accounts of the sufferings of One known as the Son of God. We can reflect on a Messiah who allowed Himself to be misunderstood, shamed, whipped, and scorned in a public execution outside the walls of Jerusalem. Today we can read about the anger of His Jewish countrymen, the flight of His friends, and the inhumanity of His Roman executioners.

The cross helps us realize that our most serious problems are not disease or bad environment. According to the New Testament, Christ died for our sins. It was on the cross that God showed He loved us enough to pay the price for the worst of our problems. It was there that He willingly suffered for our pride, our greed, our impulsiveness, our hatred, our sexual immorality, and our irreverence. On the cross, God offered a payment for our sins. In the words of the One who cried out, "My God, My God, why have You forsaken Me?" (Mk. 15:34), we hear the echo of our own eternal despair, as the eternal God tasted and swallowed death in our place.

Now when we ask God, "How have you loved us?" we have different information to work with.

How much does God love us? So much that the New Testament can say, "God demonstrates His own love toward us, in that while we were still sinners, Christ died for us" (Rom. 5:8). Through His suffering, we see the terribleness of our own rebellion. Through His pain, we see the extent of God's love for us.

But if we now have a new way to understand how God has loved us, we are also ready for a new understanding of how to accept His love.

A NEW OPPORTUNITY

While Old Testament Jews had many reasons to believe in the love of God, the cross of Christ went far beyond anything they had ever seen. When interpreted by the New Testament, the substitutionary death of Christ makes it clear that no one has to earn God's love. No one has to jump through moral hoops to earn His acceptance. No one has to solve difficult riddles to win His favor. No one has to live up to the legal requirements of the law of God. No one has to crawl on his knees to compensate for past sins. No one has to do such things, because God already loves us. He has already loved us enough to sacrifice His own Son on our behalf.

If Jesus was who He claimed to be, then the cross shows that it will take eternity to understand how much God loves us.

All that remains is for us to trust what He has done on our behalf. All we must do is believe that He has done for us what we could not do for ourselves (Rom. 4:5). The answer is found not by trying harder to please God but by trusting what Christ has done for us. God's love is offered to us in the form of a gift, not a reward (Eph. 2:8-10).

This is the salvation which, while coming through a Jewish Messiah and while being described by the mouths and pens of Hebrew prophets, is now offered freely to the whole world. It is the salvation described by a former rabbi who declared to Jew and Gentile alike,

> *"If you confess with your mouth, 'Jesus is Lord,' and believe in your heart that God raised Him from the dead, you will be saved. For it is with your heart that you believe and are justified, and it is with your mouth that you confess and are saved. As the Scripture says, 'Anyone who trusts in Him will never be put to shame.' For there is no difference between Jew and Gentile—the same Lord is Lord of all and richly blesses all who call on Him, for, 'Everyone who calls on the name of the Lord will be saved' "* (ROM. 10:9-13 NIV).

This is how much God loves us.

A NEW IDENTITY

The New Testament tells us that those who accept God's love in Christ become new people in the eyes of God. All who admit their sin and believe in Christ as their "sin bearer" are given a whole new way of thinking about themselves. They become children of God.

Having met the condition of accepting Christ as Savior, these people are in a position to enter fully into the love and acceptance of God. This doesn't mean God will never be displeased, angry, or unaccepting of self-destructive and disobedient behavior. It does mean that these behaviors will be handled on the basis of perfect family love rather than the legal judgment and condemning rejection that awaits those outside of Christ.

There is much more in this good news that is often seen or felt by those who have been raised in Christian homes or in Western culture. Full, undeserved acceptance in the love of Christ is the most profound and reassuring truth ever written.

A NEW EXAMPLE

As Christ surrendered to the pain of His cross in order to do the will of God, so we now are to surrender to the pain of whatever it takes to show our appreciation to God for all He has done for us.

The apostle Peter wrote:

> *For to this you were called, because Christ also suffered for us, leaving us an example, that you should follow His steps: "Who committed no sin, nor was deceit found in His mouth"; who, when He was reviled, did not revile in return; when He suffered, He did not threaten, but committed Himself to Him who judges righteously; who Himself bore our sins in His own body on the tree, that we, having died to sins, might live for righteousness—by whose stripes you were healed. For you were like sheep going astray, but have now returned to the Shepherd and Overseer of your souls* (1 PET. 2:21-25).

By being obedient to death, thereby fulfilling the love of God for others, Christ showed us how to walk in the love that is now ours. He gave us His example at Gethsemane, which shows us that when it comes to living in and expressing the love of God, we need to be ready to say:

- "Not my will but Your will."
- "Not my thoughts but Your thoughts."
- "Not my ways but Your ways."
- "Not my feelings but Your feelings."
- "Not my power but Your power."

This doesn't mean that we discount or deny our own thoughts or emotions in the process of pursuing God. It just means that we can't trust our own thoughts or emotions to give us an accurate view of reality. Our own thoughts and emotions only give us a picture of what is happening in us. They help us to see why we must continually measure ourselves—not by ourselves but by the Word of God and the Spirit of His grace. We can trust our own heart only as it helps us to see our need of Christ, our need of His undeserved help, and our need of His undeserved love.

A NEW ENABLEMENT

The New Testament tells us that once we have been accepted into the love of God by putting ourselves totally at the mercy of Christ, we have a new life and source of strength. God's Spirit now lives within us to make it possible for us to walk in the love of God.

While we cannot feel the Spirit, we can see the evidence of His presence in us as we begin to yield to His control. As we surrender to the teachings of Christ, we begin to discover what the apostle Paul meant when he wrote, "He who raised Christ from the dead will also give life to your mortal bodies through His Spirit who dwells in you" (Rom. 8:11).

We cannot feel the Spirit, but we can see the evidence of His presence in us as we begin to yield to His control.

When we're controlled by Christ rather than ourselves, the result is a growing evidence of love, joy, peace, patience, kindness, goodness, faithfulness, gentleness, and self-control (Gal. 5:22-23). This Spirit-filled (Spirit-controlled) life is the alternative to the anger and avoidance that marks those who have not found their security in the love of God.

A NEW SENSE OF BALANCE

Those in Christ have a new balance between "who they are in Christ" and "how they are doing as His child." On a scale of 1 to 10, every child of God is a perfect 10 when it comes to his legal position in Christ.

Because the Bible says that the believer in Christ stands accepted by God in Christ, there is nothing that will ever separate this child from the love of God. The most important eternal issues are settled once and for all (Rom. 8:28-39).

Practically speaking, the story may be somewhat different. We may be only a meager "1" or "3" when it comes to our love, or joy, or peace. Yet we can still please God in all of our incompleteness and immaturity if we are growing in the attitudes Jesus described as "blessed" in Matthew 5:1-10.

Having found legal and family acceptance through faith in Christ, we grow in that family relationship by letting Christ form a heart in us that is:

- poor in spirit, not arrogant
- sorry for sin, not proud
- meek before God, not stubborn
- hungering for righteousness, not for evil
- merciful, not critical and demanding
- pure in heart, not double-minded
- a peacemaker, not a divider

A NEW VISION

Once we begin to see how much God has already done for us in Christ, we can begin to get a sense of what is yet ahead. Once we begin to see how much God has sacrificed and suffered for us, we have reason to say with the apostle Paul, "He who did not spare His own Son, but delivered Him up for us all, how shall He not with Him also freely give us all things?" (Rom. 8:32). If God's Son died for us, He will also live for us. Even now, Jesus assures us that while being present with us through His Spirit, He is in heaven preparing a place for us, interceding for us, and acting as our Advocate.

If God has used time to bring us to the end of ourselves, to bring us to Himself, to test our faith, and to show that His ability to forgive is greater than our ability to sin, then He will use eternity to surprise us continually with the immeasurable and inexpressible extent of His love for us!

For now, we must conclude that it is His love

that causes Him to tell us to believe in His Son and to prepare expectantly for His any-moment return. It is because He loves us that He reminds us to love one another, to encourage one another, and to help one another walk a path that leaves no regrets.

It is God's love that encourages us to give up trying to trust Him in our own strength, and instead to believe that when we consciously surrender our bodies and minds to Him, He can live His life through us (Gal. 2:20; 3:2-5).

It is God's love that teaches us to believe that He calls us righteous, not when we successfully learn and obey all of His laws but rather when we believe in His Son (Rom. 4:5; Eph. 2:8-10; Ti. 3:5). He is our Mediator (1 Tim. 2:5), Advocate (1 Jn. 2:1), and Savior (1 Jn. 4:14).

It is God's love that teaches us to feel our own weakness and helplessness. It is God's love that leads us to despair of helping ourselves. It is God's love that teaches us to have no confidence in our own flesh before discovering the liberating difference that Christ can be in us (2 Cor. 3:5; 4:7).

It is God's love that calls us to a higher way of living while also assuring us that He Himself can provide the spiritual enablement for us to grow into this new way of life (1 Th. 5:24).

THREE

WHAT IS A
PERSONAL RELATIONSHIP
WITH GOD?

What does it mean when a person claims to have a personal relationship with God? Would you claim that for yourself? Does anyone really hear from God, talk to God, or have the kind of inside track with Him that would justify such a claim? At what point does claiming to be a friend of God amount to nothing more than the ultimate form of name-dropping?

It is my hope that the following pages will help to clarify this issue for you. None of us can afford to misunderstand this subject, which is as basic as it is profound.

—MARTIN R. DE HAAN II

You Mean You Hear God Speak?

"What do you mean there is no God?
I just talked to Him this morning."

This message borne by a faded bumper sticker has prompted a few smiles along the way. But not today. One car-length back, the driver of a late-model Cadillac curses under his breath about being stuck behind a sluggish Toyota in heavy traffic. He's even more irritated having to eat the fumes of a religious fanatic. He doesn't find the sticker funny or cute or even honest. He has a hard time with those who talk so casually about:

- Meeting God
- Knowing God
- Hearing God
- Talking to God
- Being led by God

It's not that the driver of the big car doesn't believe in God. Like most people, he's no atheist. He knows what the inside of a church looks like. His wife is religious. And without her knowledge, he has even asked heaven for a little consideration from time to time when facing a tough business deal or even a critical shot on the golf course. Sure he prays, but he's not about to claim that he has a personal relationship with God. He's suspicious of those who do.

THE GOD WHO LOVES

He suspects that they are indulging in the ultimate kind of name-dropping.

Yet in reflective moments he sometimes wonders if there's something he's missing. What could it mean to have a personal relationship with God?

WHERE DOES SUCH AN IDEA COME FROM?

The Bible doesn't refer to a personal relationship with God. Not in those exact words. But it does show the importance of learning to know, love, and trust a very personal God. While you won't find the words "personal relationship" in the Bible, the idea is everywhere. Page after page suggests that it is who you know that counts and that the who we need to know is God.

Jesus Himself prayed to His Father, "This is eternal life, that they may know You, the only true God, and Jesus Christ whom You have sent" (Jn. 17:3). Commenting on this verse, theologian J. I. Packer wrote, "What were we made for? To know God. What aim should we set ourselves in life? To know God. What is the 'eternal life' that Jesus gives? Knowledge of God....What is the best thing in life, bringing more joy, delight, and contentment than anything else? Knowledge of God" (*Knowing God*, InterVarsity Press, p.29).

A relationship with God is more, but not less, than any other relationship.

Many centuries earlier, the prophet Jeremiah quoted the Lord as saying, "Let not the wise man glory in his wisdom, let not the mighty man glory in his might, nor let the rich man glory in his riches; but let him who glories glory in this, that he understands and knows Me" (9:23-24).

What is a Personal Relationship with God?

In the following pages we'll see that a relationship with God has many of the same characteristics that mark a personal relationship between two friends. These factors include some degree of:

- Mutual recognition—each knows the other.
- Mutual openness—each approaches the other.
- Mutual interests—each shares with the other.
- Mutual respect—each honors the other.

Such a relationship means more than knowing of or about someone. We might say that we know the governor of California. But if the chief officer of that state can't pick us out of a crowd, if we can't get access to him, or if he has never shared our thoughts, feelings, and decisions, then we are claiming a friendship we don't really have.

A relationship with God is similar. If our friendship is real, we will welcome God into our lives. Our actions will show we believe He is the kind of person we want in our homes, in our plans, in our laughter, and in our tears.

With these possibilities in view, let's take a closer look at the marks of a personal relationship with God.

A SPIRITUAL RELATIONSHIP

There are those who say they have encountered God visibly, heard Him speak audibly, and felt His touch physically. Such experiences are possible. Both Old and New Testaments are marked by miraculous, life-changing encounters with God (Isa. 6:1-8). He has shown, through the pages of Scripture, that He is free to reveal Himself in any way He chooses.

These supernatural encounters, however, were the exception rather than the rule. While prophets like Isaiah, Moses, and Ezekiel had life-changing visions of God, they did not spend the rest of their lives teaching others to have similar experiences.

The God who made the world has no trouble being seen and heard by those who honestly want to know Him.

In some ways it would be nice to believe that a relationship with God means that we have a direct beam of heavenly light shining directly on us—illuminating our lives. But as a rule, the truth is far less dramatic.

To meet God doesn't mean we have to see Him visibly. We don't need to wait for visions or life-changing dreams. We can encounter God with the eyes of our understanding. Because He is an all-powerful, ever-present Spirit, He can reveal Himself to us at a deeper level than our physical senses. The One who made the world is more than able to give insight about Himself to anyone who wants to know the truth in order to obey it (Jn. 7:17; Eph. 1:17-18). He can also withhold light from those who are more interested in avoiding the truth than in finding it.

To hear God doesn't mean we have to hear Him audibly. There are times when we might wish God would break the silence and whisper in our ear. Or maybe we're glad He doesn't. In either case, it's not necessary for Him to do so. If we hear only silence, it is our own self-imposed silence.

For those who want to hear, God can be heard speaking constantly through the timeless wisdom of His Book. There and through nature (Ps. 19:1-11), He is always talking to us.

Our problem usually is not that God is not speaking but rather that we're not sure we want to hear what He has already said.

For that reason, we need to take seriously the words of the author of Hebrews, who wrote, "Therefore, as the Holy Spirit says: 'Today, *God is as close as a humbled heart.* if you will hear His voice, do not harden your hearts as in the rebellion' " (3:7-8). Our opportunity to hear Him on every page of the Bible is a privilege that carries a great degree of responsibility.

To be close to God is not a matter of location.
It is common to think that we must go to church
to meet God. That makes sense. We meet friends
at predetermined times and places. Yet, while God
does use scheduled services and addresses, He is
not limited to them. He promises to meet us in
places of the heart. He wants us to make our hearts
His home.

James recognized this when he said, "Draw near
to God and He will draw near to you" (Jas. 4:8).
He didn't say anything about where to go. He did-
n't tell us to find the highest hill in our area or a
quiet church sanctuary. Instead, James told us to
humble ourselves before the Lord (4:10). He gave
us reason to believe that wherever we seek Him,
the Lord will meet with us there.

David, the songwriter, king, and "man after
God's own heart," shows us why this is true. Deeply
humbled by the Lord's constant, unavoidable presence (Ps. 139:1-6), he prayed:

> *Where can I go from Your Spirit? Or where can
> I flee from Your presence? If I ascend into heaven,
> You are there, if I make my bed in hell, behold,
> You are there . . . . If I say, "Surely the darkness
> shall fall on me," even the night shall be light
> about me, indeed, the darkness shall not hide from
> You . . . . When I awake, I am still with You*
> (Ps. 139:7-8,11-12,18).

Nearness to God is not an issue of location. It
is a matter of whether we have place in our hearts
for Him.

To know God is not a matter of knowing all about Him. That might be the greatest understatement of all. To know God is not to master Him. At best, we can exclaim with the apostle Paul:

> *Oh, the depth of the riches both of the wisdom and knowledge of God! How unsearchable are His judgments and His ways past finding out! "For who has known the mind of the Lord? Or who has become His counselor?"* (ROM. 11:33-34).

Given the limitations of life, our minds can barely begin to grasp the meaning of terms that describe God—terms such as eternal, infinite, all-powerful, all-knowing, and everywhere-present. Yet, because He has made it possible to know Him, we can begin a process of discovery now that will never end.

We can know God because He has come to us, on our terms, to invite us to Himself on His terms. According to eyewitnesses of the New Testament Gospels, God revealed Himself to us in a person who walked on water, controlled the skies, healed withered limbs, restored sight, and stopped bleeding sores. He fed thousands with a small amount of food, drove out demons, raised the dead, loved deeply, and taught wisely.

Those who meet God now will have eternity to get to know Him.

Living a sinless life, He fulfilled Old Testament predictions, claimed to be the promised Messiah, and sacrificed His own life to secure forgiveness of sins for all who would trust Him. It was this person, known ever since as Jesus the Messiah, who said, "He who has seen Me has seen the Father" (Jn. 14:9).

So, according to the God's Word, a personal relationship with God is not only a spiritual relationship but also a Christ-centered relationship.

A CHRIST-CENTERED RELATIONSHIP

Mediators often play an important role in helping to resolve family, labor, and legal disputes. When emotions flare, insight is lost, communication stops, and stubbornness sets in. In such instances, an arbitrator can often bring renewed perspective and a plan for resolution.

The ultimate mediator is Christ. Nowhere is a personal go-between more needed than in resolving the conflict and estrangement between man and God. Our personal sin has dug out a chasm so deep and wide that it is impossible for any of us to "cross over" to God on our own. Without a mediator, we can never overcome the alienation of affection and disruption of communication that have come between us.

God is in some ways like a parent who watches his runaway son or daughter become hopelessly entangled with the law. As much as the parent would love to wrap his arms around the child and bring him home, he can't. The law has to be satisfied. Justice must be carried out. A debt to society must be paid, and a law must be enforced. For such a need, Christ has come to mediate peace between God and us (1 Tim. 2:5).

Words cannot do justice to the importance of the mediating role of Christ. Without His intervention on our behalf, we could never resolve our differences with God (Jn. 14:6). Without the urging of His loving Spirit, we would never want to.

Jesus deserves our unending appreciation, admiration, and affection. When He wiped out our debt to the law by absorbing our punishment, He proved Himself to be a friend without equal. When He rose from the dead to be life and help to all who trust Him,

"Jesus Christ received is holiness begun."
HUDSON TAYLOR

He gave us a basis for undying hope. When He ascended to the Father's right hand to intercede for us and to act as our personal advocate, He assured that He would provide for us what no mere religion or system of belief could ever offer. He has given Himself to be the solution to our every problem, to reveal God to us, and to lead us to a personal relationship with His Father.

Christianity is Christ. As W. H. Griffith Thomas points out in a book by that title, this is the real heart of our Christian faith. We have not been called to a system of laws, traditions, and inspirational ideas.

We haven't been called to the church, to a moral cause, or to the golden rule of Christian love. We have not even been called to the Bible. We have been called to Christ, the mediating person of whom the whole Bible speaks.

The apostle Paul understood the necessity of a Christ-centered relationship with God. In 1 Corinthians 1:1-9, he made it clear that he was not promoting a system of ideas. He was speaking of a relationship with God based on:

- Christ whom we serve (v. 1).
- Christ who sets Christians apart (v.2).
- Christ on whose name Christians call (v.2).
- Christ who is our Lord (v.2).
- Christ who gives us grace and peace (v.3).
- Christ who brought us the grace of God (v.4).
- Christ who has enriched us in every way (v.5).
- Christ who is confirmed by experience (v.6).
- Christ for whom we eagerly wait (v.7).
- Christ who will keep us to the end (v.8).
- Christ who will have His day (v.8).
- Christ to whom God has joined us (v.9).

Paul's obsession was not a system of new thought, an ethic, a teaching, a form of church organization, or a new program. It was the person he had come to know as the one mediator between God and man (1 Tim. 2:5). It was the person who had not only died to pay for Paul's sins (1 Cor. 15:3), but the person who, through His Spirit, was also living His life through Paul (Gal. 2:20) and was his very life (Phil. 1:21).

Are we as Christ-centered as Paul? Do we realize that true Christianity is found in the living person and personality of the resurrected Christ? Have we learned that Jesus Christ is and must be at the heart of a personal relationship with God? Have we realized that no matter where we look, Christ is there?

- Look back—He's our Creator (Col. 1:16).
- Look ahead—He's our Judge (2 Cor. 5:10).
- Look up—He's our Savior and Lord (Phil. 2:5-11).
- Look down—He's our Sustainer (Col. 1:17).
- Look right—He's our Teacher (Mt. 23:8).
- Look left—He's our Advocate (1 Jn. 2:1).
- Look within—He's our Life (Gal. 2:20).

There is no question that a personal relationship with God must be a Christ-centered relationship. It is Christ and Christ alone who can bring us to God, cleanse us from the constant pollution of the world, and be our ever-present Source of life and help.

It is Christ, the living Word, who reveals, defines, and expresses the personality of the Father. It is Christ who should continually be in our thoughts as Lord and Life. It is Christ who, by His Spirit, is a constant presence in and with all who have put their faith in Him (Mt. 28:19-20).

> *"Everything we know of God, and everything we need from Him, is deeply affected by our attitude toward Christ."*
>
> W. H. GRIFFITH THOMAS

A SUBMISSIVE RELATIONSHIP

Any husband who is content to be just "one of the boys" in his wife's eyes isn't much of a husband. Neither is a woman much of a wife if she is satisfied to be just "one of the girls." The intimacy of the marriage relationship carries with it a great sense of mutual commitment that will have a bearing on all of the couple's other activities and relationships.

For far greater reasons, the Designer of human personality is also not satisfied to be just "one of the gods" (Ex. 20:1-6). Yahweh, Provider and Deliverer of Israel, the God who came to us in Jesus the Messiah, will not accept a place on the shelf alongside Ra, Krishna, Moon, GM, or CBS. He has always been a jealous, possessive, commanding God. He will not share His honor with anyone else because no one else deserves that honor (Isa. 48:11).

God is to be feared more than all others. Most of us don't even like to think about things that frighten us. Whether we're talking about public speaking, high places, cramped spaces, dark nights, noises at the door, or creaks in the attic, the very thought can make us jumpy. Yet without fear, life would be very difficult. Even the animal world is endowed with an alarm and escape mechanism that provides the creature some degree of fight or flight necessary for survival.

At no time, however, is the emotion of fear more important or more neglected than when it involves our fear of God. To the extent that we know Him, we will also fear Him. Yet it is a fear, when under-stood, that calms all other fears and drives us to the Lord, not away from Him. It is a fear that teaches us to love, trust, and enjoy Him.

This fear might be described as the first step to a personal relationship with God. According to the wise man Solomon, "The fear of the Lord is the beginning of knowledge" (Prov. 1:7). In other words, the fear and knowledge of God go hand in hand.

Nothing and no one deserves to be feared more than the Lord. Not people, not governments, not disease, not death, not even Satan. Many who don't know God can't understand this. They assume that the Lord is the only one in the universe who doesn't need to be feared because He is too good and too loving to do us any harm. The ironic result is that such persons often end up missing the very love they seek because their lives are full of fear— fear of failure, fear of peo-

A relationship with God begins with a fear that will drive us to the safety, certainty, and enjoyment of His love.

ple, fear of natural disasters, and fear of accident, disease, and death (Dt. 28:58-68).

Those who really know the Lord take Him seri-ously. They realize that God expects to be listened to when He warns about moral and spiritual failure (Prov. 8:13; 16:6). He alone determines whether anything or anyone else will be allowed to touch or test us (Job 1); and most important, He alone determines where we will spend eternity (Mt. 10:28; Rev. 2:10; 20:1-15). Such authority deserves our respect and fear.

Although we reverence God and stand in awe of His great power, at the same time we can have strong confidence (Prov. 14:26). With David we can say, "I sought the Lord, and He heard me, and delivered me from all my fears" (Ps. 34:4). A couple of verses later David added, "The angel of the Lord encamps all around those who fear Him, and delivers them. Oh, taste and see that the Lord is good; blessed is the man who trusts in Him! Oh, fear the Lord, you His saints! There is no want to those who fear Him" (Ps. 34:7-9).

That comes from someone who knew his God. It comes from someone who personally experienced that the God who asks for our surrender is a God who wants us to fear Him for our own good (Jer. 32:37-39).

God is to be loved, trusted, and obeyed more than all others. Obedience, like fear, is something we tend to resist. Yet, seeing the importance of such obedience is just a matter of perspective. For example, most of us are happy to obey a stranger's directions when we're in an unknown area. We don't even think of it as obedience. We see it more like accepting help. That's the way we can look at obedience to the Lord. It is a way of accepting His help and His love that we so desperately need. Obedience is a way of showing that we really do know the Lord and that we are growing in our knowledge of how good, loving, and wise He is.

The apostle John wrote:

Now by this we know that we know Him, if we keep His commandments. He who says, "I know Him," and does not keep His commandments, is a liar, and the truth is not in him. But whoever keeps His word, truly the love of God is perfected in him. By this we know that we are in Him. He who says he abides in Him ought himself also to walk just as He walked (1 JN. 2:3-6).

The fear, trust, and obedience involved in knowing the Lord do not leave us the way we were. They make us better because Christ lives within. They change us until this relationship possesses us and dominates us—bringing us heart to heart and face to face with the God of all goodness and light.

A MUTUALLY FELT RELATIONSHIP

Roadworn, pawsore, and unnerved by children's stones and the nervous yipping insults of small pampered housedogs, the German Shepherd stray followed the stranger from a safe distance. Head low, and with an occasional look to the side, he stepped lightly and painfully in the tracks of the man who had thrown him half a bagel near the garbage bins of Ol' Blue's Diner. Cold, hungry, and longing for attention, the dog watched the stranger's every move, waiting for one more sign of recognition, the faintest chance for friendship. But it never came.

There are people who, when thinking about God, feel like this unwanted stray. They long for the assurance that God would smile and move toward them. But they assume Him to be too selective to feel anything for them. Some even see Him as an unchanging, eternal spirit who lives far above the ever-changing winds of pain and emotion that blow in and out of our lives.

But that is not true of the God of the Bible. The Scriptures assure us that He feels deeply for the most broken, roadworn, and dejected people. He cannot be touched by our strength but only by our weakness. While God's character never changes, His affections do change.

To know God is to affect Him. While God knew us, loved us, and chose us along with all His people in eternity past (Eph. 1:3-6), He relates to us personally and presently in a very intimate way. He rejoices with us when we are happy, sorrows when we are sad, and grieves when we are bad.

He has made Himself just that vulnerable to us. He has exposed His own heart to all of the loveless and heartless things that we do to Him. The Bible tells us that God can be:

- Pleased (Heb. 11:5)
- Grieved and sorrowful (Gen. 6:6; Eph. 4:30-32).
- Provoked and tested (Ps. 78:40-41).
- Burdened and wearied (Isa. 43:24).
- Angered, agitated, and furious (Ezek. 16:42-43).

Specifically, Ephesians 4:30-32 says:

Do not grieve the Holy Spirit of God, by whom you were sealed for the day of redemption. Let all bitterness, wrath, anger, clamor, and evil speaking be put away from you, with all malice. And be kind to one another, tenderhearted, forgiving one another, just as God in Christ forgave you.

The greatest evidence of His decision to make Himself vulnerable to us is found in the personal pains and sorrows of the One who with His own mind and heart revealed the Father to us. In the face of Jesus Christ, we find the face of God. He is the One who suffered for us so He could bring us to the Father. He loves us that much!

It might be hard for us to personalize that kind of love when we know we are only one in a world of more than 6 billion people. But we need to keep in mind who it is we are talking about. God does not have our limitations. He is not confined to human, one-at-a-time relationships. Rather, the One who made the world is able to relate intimately to as many of us at the same time as He desires.

How do we know God has that kind of capacity? We might come to that conclusion by reflecting on the size and complexity of the universe He created. Or we might consider the vast amounts of knowledge and information that finite people like ourselves can amass through the global Internet. Or we might simply trust the words of the One who said:

Are not two sparrows sold for a copper coin? And

not one of them falls to the ground apart from your Father's will. But the very hairs of your head are all numbered. Do not fear therefore; you are of more value than many sparrows (MT. 10:29-31).

If a sparrow doesn't fall to the ground apart from His knowledge, then the One who numbers the hairs of our head is also counting the tears, the moments of our fears, and the depth of the swirling waters threatening to engulf us.

If God knows us with this kind of knowledge, then we are never as alone as we feel. We are never without Him. We are never out of the Father's reach. Even though He might test our faith and our patience by not responding immediately in the way we want Him to, we can be reassured with a peace and confidence that can calm the turbulence within and lead to dramatic changes in us.

To know God is to be affected by Him. Think for a moment about the people who have changed your life for the better. Maybe it was the teacher who inspired you to go for your dreams. Maybe it was the parent or grandparent whose words and things made you feel deeply loved. Maybe it was the neighbor who showed you by his example that any job worth doing is worth doing well. Looking back, you can see that knowing these people changed your life.

What is true of these people will be even more true of those who come to know God. No one can know Him without being changed by Him. Anyone who comes into God's presence will be touched and changed by the One who loves us enough to accept us as we are but loves us too much to leave us that way. The apostle James described such a personal relationship with God like this:

> *Therefore submit to God. Resist the devil and he will flee from you. Draw near to God and He will draw near to you. Cleanse your hands, you sinners; and purify your hearts, you double-minded. Lament and mourn and weep! Let your laughter be turned to mourning and your joy to gloom. Humble yourselves in the sight of the Lord, and He will lift you up* (4:7-10).

To know God in this way means allowing our hearts to be broken by the things that break His heart. It means finding joy in the things that bring Him joy, discovering strength in His strength, and receiving hope in the assurance that nothing is too hard for Him. It means finding a new lease on life in One who offers us forgiveness in exchange for our repentance, comfort in

To develop a personal relationship with God means to learn to love what He loves and hate what He hates.

trade for our sorrow, and the promise of a world to come for our willingness to release our grip on this present one.

We are changed as we discover that to know God is to love Him. To love Him is to give Him first place in our hearts. Giving Him first place is to care about those He cares about, to love what He loves, to hate what He hates, and to join Him in the family business of redeeming broken lives.

This is the kind of healthy relationship that God calls us to. But such maturity doesn't just happen. Sometimes a personal relationship with God remains a faint glimmer of what it was meant to be. Sometimes we stop short of the growth to which God calls us.

A GROWING RELATIONSHIP

Who could doubt the personal relationship between parents and their newborn baby in the hospital nursery. Yet a one-sided parent-infant relationship provides an important counterbalance to much of what we've said up until now. On earlier pages we've emphasized the mutual nature of a relationship. Now we need to see the other side of this truth.

Just as some babies do not grow and thrive, many children of God follow a similar pattern. Sometimes growth starts and then stalls. Even though God Himself is committed to bring us to eventual maturity, He often allows us to remain infantile in our attitudes and knowledge of Him.

The apostle Paul addressed this issue of immaturity and lack of growth when he wrote:

I, brethren, could not speak to you as to spiritual people but as to carnal, as to babes in Christ. I fed you with milk and not with solid food; for until now you were not able to receive it, and even now you are still not able; for you are still carnal. For where there are envy, strife, and divisions among you, are you not carnal and behaving like mere men? (1 COR. 3:1-3).

Expect a process. Growing to maturity takes equal amounts of diligence and patience. On one hand, we must never be satisfied with the level of our relationship and knowledge of God. If we are, we'll stagnate, sour, and go backward. On the other hand, we must be patient with ourselves and not expect more than God expects of us.

Scripture shows that this maturity doesn't happen overnight. It requires time—time with God, and time in His Word. For that reason Peter wrote, "As newborn babes, desire the pure milk of the word, that you may grow thereby, if indeed you have tasted that the Lord is gracious" (1 Pet. 2:2-3). James supported the progressive nature of this relationship with God when he wrote:

My brethren, count it all joy when you fall into various trials, knowing that the testing of your faith produces patience. But let patience have its perfect work, that you may be perfect and complete, lacking nothing (1:2-4).

Don't rush the process. But don't let it stop. Continue to feed on the Word of God even as you allow Him to show Himself faithful in the seasons, tests, and troubles of life. Don't expect perfection. We will fail. Be content to be learning and growing. Don't be like the homeowner who planted a garden, only to dig it up 2 weeks later because he didn't have tomatoes yet.

Expect change. Because of the very nature of spiritual life, our relationship with the Lord will change. It will change because as we go forward we will always find more—more knowledge and experience of God that will stretch us, enlarge our hearts, and make us better.

Our relationship with God can also change for the worse, however, if we begin to coast and rely on past experiences with Him. We must expect change because our relationship with Him is by nature a contested issue. Our adversary, the devil, won't be satisfied until he neutralizes us and we slip into a spiritual coma (Eph. 6:10-13).

Although our personal relationship with God can never be lost, the characteristics of that relationship will change. We will change. Count on it. Our hearts will either grow warmer or colder. Our character will either deepen or thin out. Our conversations with God will either become more intimate or less meaningful and less frequent.

Allow for incompleteness. Speaking of our incomplete relationship with God, Paul said:

For we know in part and we prophesy in part. But when that which is perfect has come, then that which is in part will be done away .... For now we see in a mirror, dimly, but then face to face. Now I know in part, but then I shall know just as I also am known. And now abide faith, hope, love, these three; but the greatest of these is love (1 COR. 13:9-10,12-13).

That's the realism we face. Our knowledge and experience are incomplete. It's as if we are looking at the face of God through a clouded glass. But then it will be face to face. In the meantime, we have our orders. We must accept our incompleteness, trust God, and put our hope in His imminent return. We are to love God and His imperfect family with all of our heart. We can't afford to demand perfection of ourselves. Neither should we demand it of others. The holiness and growth that God is looking for will be seen in our brokenness and humility, not in our spiritual perfection.

Don't expect heaven now. Not only is it important for us to give ourselves time to grow in the Lord, but it is also essential that we take time to let Him show Himself absolutely faithful and satisfying to us. But don't expect in this life what He has promised to complete in eternity.

We who trust in Christ are people of eternity. There are no time limits on our future. We are not like the professional athlete who has to reach his goals and make his money and a name for himself in just a few short years before he loses his competitive edge.

Having a relationship with God is not a way to get everything we want in life. It is not the key to financial success, good health, and long life. It is, however, the way to find increasing amounts of inner love, joy, peace, patience, kindness, goodness, faithfulness, and self-control (Gal. 5:22-23). It is a means of finding the ultimate relationship, the ultimate purpose, the ultimate mission, the ultimate security, the ultimate hope.

All that remains for us is to trust Christ for what we cannot now see or have. We need to believe that what Christ said to His disciples is still true:

Let not your heart be troubled; you believe in God, believe also in Me. In My Father's house are many mansions; if it were not so, I would have told you. I go to prepare a place for you. And if I go and prepare a place for you, I will come again and receive you to Myself; that where I am, there you may be also (JN. 14:1-3).

That is our hope. We should not expect the Lord to give us everything we crave now. While He has promised to provide for the needs of all who follow Him, He also reserves the right to determine what we need now and what we will be able to enjoy more if it is deferred until later.

A SHARED RELATIONSHIP

We all come to God one at a time. In a sense, we come all alone. It is our personal decision, our choice, whether or not we are willing to enter into a personal relationship with God. No one else makes this decision for us. But it doesn't stop there.

Once we come to God, we are joined to Him and born into His family.

Those who love God will love one another. It is impossible to have a personal relationship with God without also having Christ-centered relationships with other people. Christ's love shown on the cross is our example. He showed us that to be close to the Father means to share the Father's love for others (1 Jn. 4:7-11). As I get to know the Lord, I will also be confronted with a God who dearly loves those people around me—my family, friends, neighbors, business associates, acquaintances, and even my enemies.

This is the kind of attitude Paul encouraged in the Christians at Thessalonica. After affirming the reality and evidence of their relationship to God (1 Th. 1:1-7), he went on to say:

> *Concerning brotherly love you have no need that I should write to you, for you yourselves are taught by God to love one another; and indeed you do so toward all the brethren who are in all Macedonia. But we urge you, brethren, that you increase more and more* (4:9-10).

We might like to live in isolation, but we can't do that if we're going to grow in our relationship with God. Knowing God doesn't mean just knowing about Him; it means entering into Him—into His thoughts, His heart, His sacrificial love.

The apostle John wrote:

Beloved, let us love one another, for love is of God; and everyone who loves is born of God and knows God. He who does not love does not know God, for God is love (1 Jn. 4:7-8).

Those who love God are dependent on one another. In Ephesians 4, Paul made it clear that our vertical relationship with God is accompanied by many horizontal relationships. He pictured each child of God as a member of the body of Christ. Each part has a function. Just as the eye, ear, mouth, and foot make distinct contributions to our physical bodies, so each believer plays a distinct role in the church, the body of Christ. When every part does its share, the whole body receives the benefit (see 1 Cor. 12 and Rom. 12).

Even though we have received a complete salvation in Christ, there is another sense in which we are not complete without relating to and serving one another. We need one another just as much as the mouth needs the eye and the eye needs the hand. This is the outworking of our salvation. We might think we are independent spirits who can do just fine on our own, but we will soon discard that idea as we grow in our knowledge of God.

Those who love God will submit to one another. In Ephesians 5:21, Paul said that we are to submit to one another in the fear of God. In the counsel that follows, his words become very specific:

- Wives are to serve their husbands as a means of serving the Lord (5:22).

- Husbands should lovingly surrender their own interests in behalf of their wives as Christ lovingly surrendered His interests in behalf of the church (5:25-28).
- Children are to obey their parents in the Lord (6:1).
- Servants are to be obedient to their masters as a means of serving the Lord (6:5-7).
- Masters are to show consideration for their servants out of deference to the Lord (6:9).

The message comes through clearly. Knowing God and His love (Eph. 3:14-21) means that we will lovingly and submissively serve others. As we trust God and obediently serve others, we will discover deep within our own souls the righteousness, wisdom, and power of the love of Christ.

Obediently channeling God's love to others enables us to begin to experience the meaning of Paul's prayer in Ephesians 3:14-19.

For this reason I bow my knees to the Father of our Lord Jesus Christ, from whom the whole family in heaven and earth is named, that He would grant you, according to the riches of His glory, to be strengthened with might through His Spirit in the inner man, that Christ may dwell in your hearts through faith; that you, being rooted and grounded in love, may be able to comprehend with all the saints what is the width and length and depth and height—to know the love of Christ which passes knowledge; that you may be filled with all the fullness of God.

One Who Was Close...
Yet So Far Away

It is possible to be close to Christ yet so far from the life He offers.

This was true even among the original 12 apostles of Christ. They had the most obvious opportunity for a personal relationship with Him. Yet even in that inner circle, there was one, probably the most trusted member of the group (for he kept the money), who never really had the kind of personal connection with Christ that we are talking about. Judas knew a lot about Jesus. He knew the Teacher's habits well enough to lead Jesus' enemies to a garden meeting place. He knew Christ well enough to betray Him with a kiss of greeting. But Judas didn't know Jesus as his Savior and Lord.

Trusted though he was, the "keeper of the money" never had the kind of personal, Christ-centered relationship with God that is available to us today. He is a troubling example of the kind of person Jesus talked about when He said:

Enter by the narrow gate; for wide is the gate and broad is the way that leads to destruction. . . . Many will say to Me in that day, "Lord, Lord, have we not prophesied in Your name, cast out demons in Your name, and done many wonders in Your name?" And then I will declare to them, "I never knew you; depart from Me, you who practice lawlessness!" (MT. 7:13,22-23).

Let's make sure that we do not end up as one who presumed that to know about Christ is to know Him personally.

Making It Personal

Someone has said, "Knowing Christ died—that's history. Believing He died for me—that's salvation." A personal relationship with Christ begins at the moment of our salvation. Jesus referred to this event as a second birth (Jn. 3:3). Only when we are born spiritually into God's family do we become His children, His friends, His servants, and members of His spiritual kingdom.

While we may not know exactly when this new life begins, we can understand the steps we need to take to begin this relationship.

FIRST STEP:
We need to admit our lost condition.

All of us are born to the parents of a fallen humanity. We come into this world separated from the life of God and absorbed with an interest in finding satisfaction, significance, and personal independence on our own terms. In the process, we don't show a natural desire for God, who made us for Himself (Rom. 3:11-12).

While we may look good to ourselves as long as we measure ourselves by ourselves, Jesus Christ showed us our sin. He is the One who showed us what it means to have a personal relationship with

God. He is also the One who said that He didn't come into this world to help good people, but "to seek and to save that which was lost" (Lk. 19:10).

The Bible says we all come into this physical world physically alive but spiritually dead—missing out on the quality of life for which God made us. The apostle Paul wrote, "All have sinned and fall short of the glory of God" (Rom. 3:23), "There is none righteous, no, not one" (Rom. 3:10), and "The wages of sin is death" (Rom. 6:23).

SECOND STEP:
We need to know what God has done for us.

The word *gospel* means "good news." The gospel of Christ is that God loved us enough to send His own Son into this world to rescue us from ourselves and our sin (Jn. 1:1-4; 3:16).

The good news is that Jesus lived the quality of life that God intended for us to live. Without flaw, He loved His heavenly Father with all of His heart, soul, and mind. Without fail, He showed us what it means to love our neighbor as ourselves.

Then, to solve the problem of our lost relationship with His Father, Jesus died in our place, offering Himself as a perfect sacrifice to pay the price of sin. Because He was not only man but also God our Creator (Jn. 1:1-14), His death was of infinite value. When He rose from the dead, He proved that He had died in our place to pay the price of all sin—past, present, and future. With one sacrifice, He paid for the least—and the worst—of our sin.

THIRD STEP:
We need to personally believe and receive God's gift.

While we all have earned the wages of spiritual death and separation from God (Rom. 6:23), no one can earn a relationship with God. It is a gift of His love and mercy—not a reward for our effort. No one is saved by trying to be good. We are saved by trusting in Christ.

This is why the apostle Paul could write, "For by grace [undeserved favor] you have been saved through faith, and that not of yourselves; it is the gift of God, not of works, lest anyone should boast" (Eph. 2:8-9; see also Rom. 4:5; Ti. 3:5).

Knowing Christ died— that's history. Believing that He died for me—that's salvation.

This may sound too simple. But it takes a miracle of God's grace to break our pride and self-sufficiency. It takes God's Spirit to draw us into this kind of personal relationship. If this is your desire, this is how you can begin.

The actual words we say to God to receive this gift may vary (Lk. 18:13; 23:42-43). What is important is that we believe God enough to be able to say, "Father, I know I have sinned against You. I believe that Jesus is Your Son, that He died for my sins, and that He rose from the dead to prove it. Now I accept Your offer of eternal life. I accept Jesus as Your gift for my salvation."

If this is the honest expression of your heart, welcome to God's family! By simple, childlike faith you have entered into a personal relationship with the One who made you and saved you for Himself.

Power for Living

Every child of God is to grow spiritually. The following **POWER** acrostic will help you remember the essential elements to spiritual progress.

PRAY. Christians who want to grow, communicate with God through prayer. They express their gratitude to Him, confess their sins, and come to Him with their requests. God promises to be near to all who come to Him in prayer (Ps. 145:18).

OBEY. In John 14, Jesus said our obedience to His commands is an indicator of our love for Him (vv. 15,21,23). We can't do it in our own strength, however. That's one reason He gave us the Holy Spirit (vv. 16-17). As we yield to Him, the Spirit provides the power to walk in obedience (Gal. 5:16-25).

WORSHIP. As Christians, our devotion to God is to be continuous. Privately, we should worship God in our thoughts and prayers (Ps. 34:1). Publicly, we should unite with fellow believers in a local assembly to praise God (Ps. 111:1, Heb. 10:24-25).

EVANGELIZE. The good news of the gospel is to be shared. As we tell others what Christ has done for us, we will find ourselves growing by spiritual leaps and bounds (Mt. 28:19-20).

READ. The most direct source of a Christian's spiritual growth is the Bible. It must be read regularly because it is our milk and strong meat (1 Pet. 2:2; Heb. 5:12-14). It tells us how to live (Ps. 119:105). It is God's word to us today.

FOUR

HOW
DOES GOD
KEEP HIS
PROMISES?

What if we have done our part by "believing," but we haven't seen any results? Is there something we don't understand? Is there something else we need to do to see God's promises fulfilled?

If you are searching for answers to these kinds of questions, I encourage you to read the following pages. This chapter, written by Kurt De Haan, guides us through a study of what the Bible says about the promises of God. Use this material as a starting point for your own discovery of the vast wealth of promises we have been given by a faithful God.

—MARTIN R. DE HAAN II

But You Promised!

Have people ever let you down? That question belongs in the same category as: Do birds have wings? Do fish have fins? Is the sun hot? Is water wet?

But what about this question: Has God ever let you down? What if we rephrase it: Have you ever felt that God didn't keep His word? Think about it for a minute. Have you wondered, even complained, that He didn't come through the way you thought He said He would?

We know, for instance, that God has promised to protect and care for His children in this world. He has promised to make them strong, to fill their hearts with joy and a peace that passes all understanding. We know that God has promised to answer our prayers.

Yet at times those promises seem empty. Our prayers for a rebellious child or an unsaved spouse seem to go unanswered. A friend dies of cancer. Inflation chews at our paycheck. Neighborhood crime gets worse. Terrorists plague the world. And Jesus hasn't come back yet.

What happened to all the promises? Has God failed to keep His word? Have our expectations exceeded God's promises?

WHAT IS A PROMISE?

The way some people use the term, a promise is nothing more than a good intention—easily discarded if it gets in the way. They see a promise as something that is made to be broken. But when God makes a promise, He's doing more than just expressing wishful thinking. He is giving His absolutely trustworthy word!

The original language of the Old Testament does not have a specific word for the concept of promise, but that doesn't mean the idea isn't there. The Hebrew words (*amar, dabar*) that are translated by the English word *promise* have the meaning of "to say" or "to speak." When God and others in the Bible speak about what they will do in the future, the word *promise* fits well. In each case, the speaker's word, honor, and integrity are at stake.

> *The promises of God are the heart of the Bible.*

The New Testament follows the same pattern as the Old. God stands behind what He says. Therefore the idea comes naturally from the Greek word *angelia*, which means "an announcement" or "a message."

The promises of God are the heart of the Bible. Everything God has spoken, every announcement, every message, is really a promise based on God's perfect, good, and trustworthy character.

WHY IS THERE CONFUSION ABOUT THE WAY GOD KEEPS HIS PROMISES?

At times, a gap develops between what we think God has said He would do and what we see happening in our everyday experience. This gap, however, says more about our failure to understand than about God's ability to remain true. Our confusion can be due to any one (or several) of the following factors.

1. Faulty expectations. At times we may fall into the trap of thinking that God will keep His promises in the way we expect. We might assume that He will do it in ways that are immediately obvious rather than in a manner that becomes apparent only in time. We may expect Him to change our external circumstances and environment when what He really wants us to see is that His promises can be fulfilled through inner changes in us.

We tend to be shortsighted. God is into long-range planning. We see only the surface, here-and-now events, and we do not know how God is working behind the scenes to fit the pieces together to form an overall pattern. The ways God has acted in the past, though, show that He fulfills some promises in stages or in unexpected ways.

2. Faulty interpretations and applications. We may simply miss the point of what God has said. Or we may understand a biblical promise accurately but fail to see that God gave the promise to someone else in a particular situation.

A small book of collected biblical promises states in the introduction: "Take each promise to mean just exactly what it says. Don't try to interpret it or add to it or read between the lines." That may sound good. We certainly must avoid reading "between the lines" of Scripture, but it is dangerous to say that we should not try to interpret the promises. That can be a huge mistake. Failure to understand a promise in its context can lead to some very bad conclusions. Too many people go around quoting Bible verses as promises to them as individuals when in fact the promises were given to specific biblical characters, a nation, or only to people of a certain time period.

3. Faulty feelings. Our emotions have a way of taking over the driver's seat of our lives. Wrong emotions can overrule right thinking. As a result, if we have been hurt, we blame God for not doing what we think He promised. The death of a loved one can cause us to lose perspective if we allow our feelings to override the truth about God. A failed romance or a marriage on the rocks can trigger doubts. Personal rejection, failure, loss of a job, physical pain, or injustice can stir up feelings against God that become stronger than any force of reason.

4. Faulty memory. When it comes to remembering, we can all be like an absent-minded professor who forgets how to get home. We can get so wrapped up in the details of everyday life that we forget more than just anniversaries, birthdays, phone calls, groceries, and appointments. We even forget what should mean the most to us—the evidence of God's faithfulness in our lives and how He has fulfilled His promises to us in the past. As a result, we lose confidence in His ability to be faithful in the future.

So now what do we do? How do we bring our expectations and feelings in line with God's plans and truths? How do we live a fulfilling life by faith in God's promises? That's what the following pages will try to resolve.

How Does God Keep His Promises?

Every political campaign seems to be the same. Promises and platitudes pollute the air. (Maybe that's what is depleting the earth's ozone layer!) Each candidate tries to out-promise the other. And after every election, the results are predictably the same.

Some promises are quickly broken because the candidate never intended to fulfill them. Other promises, while well-intentioned, were beyond the candidate's power and ability to fulfill. Maybe an unforeseen string of events or new information changed the politician's mind about the wisdom of his original statement. Powerful special-interest groups may exert pressure, making sure that they get what was promised, while less influential people seem to get lost in the crowd.

God, though, is not like a politician, a corporate executive, a supervisor, a teacher, a student, an employee, a coach, a player, a father, a mother, or a child. Everybody—not just the politician—has a problem with keeping promises. We all have difficulty following through on our word. God, however, does not. He has all the power and wisdom in the universe at His disposal. He will never have to make an excuse for failing to fulfill what He has promised, and we have no excuse for not believing Him.

We've already mentioned some possible reasons for the seeming gap between our perceptions of God's promises and how life actually is played out. Together, let us search for answers that will help us correct our view of God and His promises. We will discover that God keeps His promises (1) on His terms, (2) to His intended audience, (3) by His methods, and (4) in His time.

ON HIS TERMS

Do you read product labels? If you do, you've read words like these: "This product is guaranteed for 5 years from date of purchase against defects in workmanship. The guarantee excludes damage caused by failure to follow label directions." Or you've read a recipe in a cookbook that guarantees a delicious dessert—if you follow the directions. You can't get away with substituting baking soda for flour, or salt for sugar.

God's terms for keeping His advertised promises are clearly stated. And what He promises, He will deliver. Some promises come with an unconditional guarantee. That is, He promises to hold up His end of the agreement no matter what we do. Then there are promises that carry with them directions (conditions) that we must follow if we are to enjoy all that He has offered. These conditional promises are dependent on our fulfilling certain requirements.

Psalm 100 reminds us of the character qualities of the One who makes promises on His terms:

> *Know that the Lord, He is God; it is He who has made us, and not we ourselves; we are His people and the sheep of His pasture. Enter into His gates with thanksgiving, and into His courts with praise. Be thankful to Him, and bless His name. For the Lord is good; His mercy is everlasting, and His truth endures to all generations (vv. 3-5).*

The One who made us continues to be the Lord over all of life. By His nature God is good, merciful, and forever true to His word. The rest of the Bible tells us how God's promises to mankind reflect those qualities. Because He is all those things, we do not have to fear when we hear that God keeps His promises on His terms.

What kinds of conditions are attached to God's promises? Many promises are like appliance warranties that hold true only if the customer does not do things that void the agreement. That was the case in the Garden of Eden. God promised that Adam and Eve would enjoy life in the Garden if they followed His rules, but they would suffer the death penalty if they disobeyed (Gen. 2:16-17).

The covenant that God made with Moses and the people of Israel at Mount Sinai contained many conditions. Prior to the giving of the Ten Commandments, God said to Israel that if they kept the covenant agreement with Him and obeyed Him fully, He would care for them as His special treasure (Ex. 19:3-6).

The Ten Commandments state a few results of missing or meeting God's conditions. The Lord said that He would punish all who worshiped idols, but He would show love to those who loved Him (Ex. 20:4-6). He promised to hold guilty anyone who spoke His name in a disrespectful or contemptuous way (v.7). He promised long life in the Promised Land to those who honored their parents (v.12).

In Exodus 23:20-33, God said He would wipe out Israel's enemies when they went into Palestine, He would take away sickness, and He would ensure long life and no miscarriages. However, the conditions included paying attention to and obeying the Angel of God, worshiping God, and not making a covenant with their enemies or allowing them to live in the Promised Land.

Here are some other examples of *conditional* Old Testament promises:

- God promised success, prosperity, and protection *if* the people obeyed the Law of Moses (Josh. 1:7-9).
- God told Gideon that *if* he followed His directions, he would win a battle (Judg. 7:1-25).
- God told Eli that His previous promise to bless his family and maintain his family priesthood was going to be nullified *because* of the sins of Eli and his sons (1 Sam. 2:27-36).
- When the Israelites asked for a king, the Lord promised good things *if* the people honored and obeyed Him, but He warned of

judgment *if* they rebelled (1 Sam. 12:13-15).

- *Because* Saul failed to measure up to God's demands, he forfeited the kingship (1 Sam. 13:13-14).
- *If* a person takes his advice from the Lord and not from wicked people, he will enjoy the Lord's favor (Ps. 1).
- A person can enjoy a close relationship with God *if* he does what is right, speaks the truth, does no wrong to his neighbor, despises the vile person, honors the righteous, keeps his word, and does not exploit others (Ps. 15).
- *If* a person puts his trust in the Lord and follows obediently, he will experience the shepherding love of God (Ps. 23).
- *If* you "delight . . . in the Lord," then "He shall give you the desires of your heart" (Ps. 37:4).
- *If* a person reveres God, he will find wisdom and gain God's blessing (Prov. 2:1-8; 3:1-10).
- Isaiah reminded the people of the Lord's desire to give them the best He had to offer— *if* they would only obey Him (Isa. 1:10-20).
- Ezekiel said that a person could expect judgment *if* he were guilty and honor *if* he were righteous (Ezek. 18).
- Jonah announced judgment on Nineveh *if* the people did not repent (Jon. 3).

Here are some examples of New Testament conditions:

- God will bless *if* we become poor in spirit,

mourn over sin, express meekness, hunger and thirst for righteousness, show mercy, seek purity, pursue peace, or experience persecution for God's sake (Mt. 5:1-12).

- *If* we seek what has eternal value, God will take care of our temporal needs (Mt. 6:25-34).
- *If* we put our trust in Jesus, we will be given eternal life; but *if* we reject Him, we cannot escape condemnation (Jn. 3:16-18).
- *If* we submit to God and resist the devil, he will flee from us (Jas. 4:7).
- God has given us everything we need to live in a way that pleases Him. *If* we take hold of what He has given to us, we will "never stumble" and we will be rewarded in heaven (2 Pet. 1:3-11).
- God will forgive *if* we confess (1 Jn. 1:9).
- *If* we ask anything according to God's will, we will receive what we pray for (1 Jn. 5:14-15).

What kinds of promises are unconditional?
An unconditional promise is simply one in which God says He will do something, and nothing we can do will stop it from happening. The fulfillment of unconditional promises does not depend on the faithfulness of people but only on God. Even if we are unfaithful, God cannot be anything but faithful to His word (2 Tim. 2:13).

Here are some examples of *unconditional* promises:

- God told Noah that He would never again send a worldwide flood (Gen. 9:8-17).
- God promised Abraham a son, a nation from

his descendants, and a land (Gen. 15).

- David received assurance that his royal line would last forever (2 Sam. 7:16).
- God repeatedly told Israel of His unfailing love for them and His ultimate plan to restore their nation (Jer. 30–33).
- Jesus said He would return to earth to reward the righteous and punish the wicked (Mt. 16:27; 25:31-46).
- Jesus promised that after He ascended to heaven He would send the Holy Spirit (Jn. 16:5-15).
- Jesus said that Satan's forces would never overcome the church (Mt. 16:18).
- Jesus promised to save, keep, and resurrect to eternal life all who trust in Him (Jn. 6:35-40).

Can God's promises ever be only partially fulfilled? Yes. Some promises may be fulfilled in part because only part of the conditions have been met, or the promises may be fulfilled in stages according to God's plan.

For example, the Lord told the Jewish people who were coming out of Egypt that He would drive out the nations before them and give them the Promised Land. They were to do this in stages (Dt. 7:22), but because of their failure to follow all His instructions they only drove out part of the people who inhabited the land, and they experienced only part of God's blessing.

Another good example is the group of prophecies about the coming Messiah. The Old Testament promises were fulfilled in part during Christ's first coming, and the others will be fulfilled when He comes again. The prophets spoke of a coming king who would be of the line of David, a king who would restore Israel's status as God's special nation (Isa. 9:6-7; 11; Jer. 33:14-26; Zech. 9:9-10). Jesus fulfilled the part of the promise about the suffering Servant (Isa. 53), and He will one day return to set up His eternal kingdom.

Should Proverbs be interpreted as promises?

The proverbs are promises in the broad sense that they describe how God rewards those who fear Him and live wisely, and how He opposes those who disregard Him and live foolishly. We can run into problems, however, if we do not interpret the proverbs within the context of Old Testament wisdom writings and in light of all biblical truths.

The proverbs offer practical wisdom about the effects of certain kinds of actions. For example, a person who lives a life of violence can expect to be a victim of violence (1:18-19). Ignoring the wisdom of the proverbs will lead to a shortened, problem-filled life (1:19-33) instead of a life that enjoys the favor of God (3:1-8). Not every proverb, though, can be understood as a promise of here-and-now results. Within the context of the whole Bible, we know that in many cases God reserves the right to delay perfect justice until the day of judgment.

Many verses in Proverbs 3 seem to promise wealth, health, safety, and happiness to those who follow the path of wisdom. Proverbs 10:3 says that the righteous person will not go hungry. A righteous person will be untouched by trouble, according to 19:23. No one would deny that these proverbs do reflect the general principles of how God has designed life to operate—we reap what we sow (Prov. 11:24-26; 22:8-9; 2 Cor. 9:6; Gal. 6:7). But life is not always so predictable—as the experiences of Job, David, Solomon, the apostle Paul, and other Bible characters demonstrate. In many cases, God has something better in store for a person than immediate here-and-now blessings—such people are laying up treasure in heaven.

The proverbs, therefore, provide down-to-earth principles for everyday life. The person who wants to be wise and enjoy God's favor will read the proverbs and put their God-fearing instruction into practice.

Thinking It Over
How is God's ability to keep His promises different from our ability to keep our promises? Why does God keep His promises? Are you enjoying the full benefits of God's promises, or are there conditions that you are not meeting?

TO HIS INTENDED AUDIENCE

Has this ever happened to you? As you pull the envelope out of your mailbox, you read: "You are the winner of 10 million dollars . . . ." For a moment you don't know whether to jump up and down or to call all your relatives. But when sanity returns, you decide to open the envelope first. When you do, you notice how the sentence continues (in smaller print of course): "... if your numbers match those selected by the sweepstakes computer." The promise of 10 million dollars applies only to the one person who received the right numbers.

When you read the Bible and you come across a statement that sounds like it would be a great promise, can you claim it for yourself? Maybe you are unemployed, having a hard time making your savings stretch, and you open your Bible to the place where God gives a great promise about being prosperous and living in a land flowing with milk and honey. Would you get excited? You might if you didn't read on to learn that the promise was intended for Israel prior to occupying the Promised Land, not you and your desire to move to Beverly Hills. Although such a promise is limited to whom it is addressed, it does reflect God's ability to prosper anyone He chooses to prosper.

The author of Psalm 145 recognized that while some of God's good promises apply to all people, other promises apply only to a select person or group:

The Lord is good to all, and His tender mercies are over all His works. . . . You open Your hand and satisfy the desire of every living thing. . . . The Lord is near to all who call upon Him, to all who call upon Him in truth. He will fulfill the desire of those who fear Him; He also will hear their cry and save them. The Lord preserves all who love Him, but all the wicked He will destroy (Ps. 145:9,16,18-20).

Before we can claim one of God's promises, we need to know if He is talking to us or not.

What has God promised to all people? A few of the promises that apply to all inhabitants of the earth include the following: salvation to those who believe and condemnation to all who reject Christ (Jn. 3:16-18); the assurance that the earth will never again be destroyed by a flood (Gen. 9:11); a continuation of the cycles of nature as long as the earth exists (Gen. 8:22); history that will culminate according to God's master plan (Dan. 7–12); a day of judgment for believers (2 Cor. 5:10) and unbelievers (Rev. 20:11-15); a promise that God's character will not change (1 Sam. 15:29; Mal. 3:6; Jas. 1:17); rewards for all who diligently seek Him (Heb. 11:6); and the certainty that everything He says will happen will happen (Mt. 5:18; 24:34-35).

What has God promised to all believers? Second Peter 1:3-4 states:

> [God's] *divine power has given to us all things that pertain to life and godliness, through the knowledge of Him who called us by glory and virtue, by which have been given to us exceedingly great and precious promises.*

Among those great promises (conditional and unconditional) are the following:
- Provision for our needs (Mt. 6:25-34).
- Answer to prayer (Mt. 7:7-11; 1 Jn. 5:14-15).
- All we need to live for Him (2 Pet. 1:3-4).

- Rewards for service (2 Cor. 5:10).
- Help in our praying (Rom. 8:26).
- Eternal life (Jn. 3:16; 5:24).
- A home in heaven (Jn. 14:1-4).
- Assurance of salvation (Jn. 10:29).
- The Holy Spirit within (Eph. 1:13-14).
- Spiritual gifts (Rom. 12:3-8; 1 Cor. 12).
- Forgiveness for daily sins (1 Jn. 1:9).
- Peace of mind (Phil. 4:7).
- A way to defeat temptation (1 Cor. 10:13).
- Wisdom in times of testing (Jas. 1:5).
- Power for living (Eph. 1:19; 3:20).
- Access to God through prayer (Eph. 3:12).
- Mercy and grace in times of need (Heb. 4:16).
- The illumination of the Spirit (1 Cor. 2:6-16).
- Freedom from sin's grip (Rom. 6:22).
- Loving discipline (Heb. 12:3-11).
- Ability to make Satan flee (Jas. 4:7).
- Resurrection to glory (1 Th. 4:16-17).
- Strength to do God's will (Phil. 4:13).

What has God promised to Israel? The history of that nation has been one of repeated promises and the people's failure to benefit from God's gracious offers. The entire Old Testament—the books of Moses, the Writings, and the Prophets—are full of promises. The promises come in the form of assurances of God's love and care for them, as well as prophetic statements about Israel's future and the future of the surrounding nations. Here are a few of the many promises to Israel: possession of the land of Palestine (Gen. 13:14-17); the Law's blessings and curses (Dt. 28); judgment, exile, restoration (the Prophets); a Messiah (Isa. 52–53).

What has God promised to specific individuals? Many biblical promises have application to only one individual or a specific group. Here are a few examples:

- Pre-flood inhabitants: death (Gen. 6).
- Noah and his family: rescue (Gen. 7:1).
- Abram: descendants (Gen. 12:1-3; 15:1-6).
- Jacob's family: blessings (Gen. 28:10-16).
- Jews: a land of "milk and honey" (Ex. 3:8).
- Moses: miraculous signs (Ex. 4:1-17).
- Pharaoh and his people: plagues (Ex. 5–14).
- Joshua: a dry path through a river (Josh. 3).
- Gideon: victory in battle (Jud. 6:16).
- Saul: abilities needed as king (1 Sam. 10:6).
- David: a son to build the temple (2 Sam. 7).
- Solomon: wisdom and riches (1 Ki. 3:10-14).
- Hezekiah: 15 more years of life (2 Ki. 20:5-6).
- Mary: a supernatural conception (Lk. 1:26-38).
- Disciples: Spirit-aided memory (Jn. 14:26).
- Paul: strength to endure infirmities (2 Cor. 12:9).

Even though some promises were given to specific people, can't the principles apply to us? In some cases yes, and in other cases no. If the promise reflects an unchanging characteristic of God and how He relates to us, then we can reasonably assume that because He is unchanging (Jas. 1:17) He will continue to reflect that promise in relating to other people. For example, when the Lord told the apostle Paul, "My strength is made perfect in weakness." He was addressing a specific situation in Paul's life—the "thorn in the flesh" of 2 Corinthians 12:7-10. Yet that truth applies to all people who recognize their weakness and reach out to God for strength (Eph. 1:19).

An example of a promise that we cannot rightfully claim is the one given to Joshua when the Lord said, "I will give you every place where you set your foot" (Josh. 1:3 NIV). That might sound like a great promise to claim if we were looking for a home and didn't have enough money, but we would be out of order to do so. That promise could remind us that God can give us anything He in His wisdom and power chooses to give us—including a home we could afford.

Thinking It Over

What is the danger of claiming for ourselves the promises that were given specifically to other people? Take time to reread the above list of promises given to believers. Thank the Lord for what He has promised. Can you think of other biblical promises that God has given to you?

BY HIS METHODS

While we sit and scratch our heads trying to figure out how God is going to answer a prayer or fulfill His promises, He is calmly and powerfully working out His plans, often behind the scenes of life and in ways and for reasons we cannot comprehend.

In Isaiah 55, the Lord described our inability to

understand His methods. He said:

> *"My thoughts are not your thoughts, nor are your
> ways My ways," says the Lord. "For as the heavens
> are higher than the earth, so are My ways higher
> than your ways, and My thoughts than your
> thoughts. For as the rain comes down, and the snow
> from heaven, and do not return there, but water the
> earth, and make it bring forth and bud, that it may
> give seed to the sower and bread to the eater, so shall
> My word be that goes forth from My mouth; it
> shall not return to Me void, but it shall accomplish
> what I please, and it shall prosper in the thing for
> which I sent it"* (vv.8-11).

Although His reasons may elude us, and His
methods may surprise us, God always fulfills His
promises. As the apostle Paul said:

> *The foolishness of God is wiser than men, and the
> weakness of God is stronger than men* (1 COR. 1:25).

**In what obvious ways does God fulfill His
promises?** Most of the promises and prophecies
of the Bible have already been fulfilled. In many
cases the fulfillment of the promise was clear and
undeniable, just as expected.

When God told Pharaoh that He was going to
send a plague of frogs, He did just that (Ex. 8).
When the Lord told David that his son would build
the temple, Solomon was born and he later built it
(2 Sam. 7:1-17; 1 Kin. 5–8). When God said that
Judah would be judged for her unfaithfulness and
be sent into exile, that is what happened (Jer. 25).

God promised a Messiah-Savior, and Jesus came (Isa. 53; Mt. 1). Jesus said the temple would be destroyed, and in AD 70 it was demolished (Mt. 24:2). Jesus promised to build His church, and it has been growing ever since (Mt. 16:18). Jesus promised to send the Holy Spirit, and on the Day of Pentecost the Spirit came (Jn. 14:16-17; Acts 2:1-4). God told the apostle Paul that He would protect him while he was ministering in Corinth, and Paul was not harmed (Acts 18:9-11).

The Bible is full of promises that were fulfilled in obvious ways, just as one would expect. At other times, though, God's methods are a little harder to understand.

In what mysterious ways does God fulfill His promises? Sometimes we may have a hard time recognizing how God has fulfilled a promise or imagining how He will fulfill a promise.

When God promised in the Old Testament that He would send a Messiah, few people expected a Messiah like Jesus. No one could have predicted the way God brought both Jew and Gentile together into the body of Christ, the church. No one anticipated such a long time between Messiah's work as Redeemer and His work as Judge and King.

On many different occasions, the apostle Paul used the word *mystery* to describe the way God's plan of salvation has been fulfilled in Christ. The Lord revealed these truths: the inclusion of both Jew and Gentile in fulfilling God's promises of salvation (Rom. 11:25; Eph. 3:2-6), the manner in which Jesus provided forgiveness of sins (Rom. 16:25; Col. 1:24-27), the resurrection of believers in glorified bodies (1 Cor. 15:51-54), the glory of the indwelling Christ (Col. 1:27), and the establishment of the church as central to God's plan to fulfill His promises (Eph. 3:8-10).

At the center of God's mysterious fulfillment of promises about our salvation, our present life, and the life to come is Jesus Christ. Second Corinthians 1:20 states:

All the promises of God in Him are Yes, and in Him Amen, to the glory of God through us.

Jesus Christ fulfills the heart of all that "the Law of Moses and the Prophets and the Psalms" spoke about (Lk. 24:44). The Old and the New Covenant promises are based on and find their fulfillment in what Christ has done and will do (Rom. 9–11; Gal. 3–5; Heb. 7–10).

How are some promises fulfilled in ways we may not expect? At times in the Old Testament, the Lord used means that people could understand. He would send them into battle with a promise of victory, and He would give the strength to overcome an enemy. On other occasions, though, He would do something very unexpected. For example, the defeat of Pharaoh's army as they pursued the escaping Jews (Ex. 14), the collapse of the walls of Jericho (Josh. 6), and the killing of 185,000 Assyrians by the angel of the Lord (2 Ki. 19:35) demonstrated God's ability to fulfill His promises in unexpected and supernatural ways.

Another example, this time from the New Testament, shows how some promises are fulfilled differently than we might have predicted. Jesus told His disciples:

> *Assuredly, I say to you, there are some standing here who shall not taste death till they see the Son of Man coming in His kingdom* (MT. 16:28).

Six days later Jesus took Peter, James, and John with Him up a mountain. There Jesus' appearance changed, and the disciples caught a glimpse of Christ's coming glory (17:1-8). They saw a partial fulfillment of what would be completely fulfilled in the future when Jesus would come in His glory to establish His rule over all the earth.

How does God fulfill some promises in a spiritual way? Although God sometimes fulfills promises in visible ways, at other times He demonstrates His faithfulness by providing invisible, spiritual blessings.

The Psalms contain many statements about the power of God to bless the righteous with protection, wealth, health, and long life. We would be wrong, though, to conclude that we can expect nothing but physical prosperity in this life. One look at the life of David contradicts that idea. His life was one of repeated conflict and ups and downs of physical well-being.

It is true that we will reap what we sow (Gal. 6:7-8), but that does not mean that we will reap all the benefits right now, in this life, in physical, tangible ways. Job knew that. His friends, though, made the mistake of assuming that right living always translates into a trouble-free life right here and now. Or look at the life of the apostle Paul. He went through all types of good and bad experiences, yet he found that in all of life he could be content because God was being faithful to him (Phil. 4:11-13).

My wife made a plaque for my office with the words of Isaiah 40:28-31 written on it. Verse 31 states:

> *Those who wait on the Lord shall renew their strength; they shall mount up with wings like eagles, they shall run and not be weary, they shall walk and not faint.*

Since I like to jog regularly, it would be great if I could take those words to mean strength for running a 25K race without getting tired. But the Lord was not speaking to me about running in a physical sense. What those poetic verses promise, however, is God's strength to do what He wants you and me to do. In that sense, the words are echoed by Paul's statement: "I can do all things through Christ who strengthens me" (Phil. 4:13). The fulfillment of the promise in Isaiah 40, then, comes primarily through the provision of inner spiritual strength.

Thinking It Over
What kind of conclusion did Job come to after he had questioned God's method of dealing with him? (Job 42:1-3). Why do we sometimes have trouble understanding God's methods of keeping His promises? How have God's promises been fulfilled in your life?

IN HIS TIME

Preschool children have trouble comprehending time. You can't tell a child, "We're going to the zoo in 2 weeks," and not expect him to ask you every day for the next 2 weeks if "today" is the day to go to the zoo.

Adults also have trouble with time. We have difficulty understanding God's timing and how He fulfills His promises. We can't wait. We expect results today or tomorrow, not years from now.

The author of Ecclesiastes, however, put God's timing into proper perspective. He wrote:

> To everything there is a season, a time for every purpose under heaven . . . . [God] has made everything beautiful in its time. Also He has put eternity in their hearts, except that no one can find out the work that God does from beginning to end . . . . God shall judge the righteous and the wicked, for there is a time there for every purpose and for every work (3:1,11,17).

In Ecclesiastes 3, the writer points out that the time-bound people of planet earth cannot grasp God's eternal purposes (v. 11). The perpetual changes of life are part of God's pattern, His plan for all the ages. From the human perspective, though, it looks like a bunch of tangled thread on the back of a piece of tapestry. We cannot see how God is working it all together.

As a result, we sometimes question God's timing. If we don't see His promises becoming reality right now, we become impatient. We need to teach ourselves that God's timing is best.

How does God delay in keeping His promises?
Hebrews 11 gives us a sampling of Old Testament saints who came to realize that God fulfills His promises according to His time plan. They lived by faith, believing that God would eventually do all He promised, even if they did not understand why the Lord delayed action for several years or beyond their lifetime.

Abraham is the preeminent example in Hebrews 11. When God told him to pack his bags and travel to the land of promise, Abraham went, though he didn't know where he was going. The Lord told Abraham that he and Sarah would have a child, yet the Lord waited until their old age to fulfill His word. And Abraham had to imagine the future when his descendants would inherit the Promised Land.

Isaac, Jacob, and Joseph knew of God's promise for their descendants, but they did not see fulfillment (vv.20-22). Moses knew that the Lord would rescue His people, but he had to wait until he was 80 years old before the Lord used him to lead the people out of Egypt. Moses even chose mistreatment in the short run so that later He would be rewarded by God (vv.25-26).

The writer of Hebrews 11 also lists Gideon, Barak, Samson, Jephthah, David, Samuel, and the prophets. Their lives were a combination of immediate blessing and delayed fulfillment.

Verses 33 through 35 list several ways in which they saw God's blessings. But verses 35 through 38 list the terrible torture, imprisonment, and death that many faced. And then the chapter ends with these words:

> All these, having obtained a good testimony through faith, did not receive the promise, God having provided something better for us, that they should not be made perfect apart from us (VV. 39-40).

The writer of Hebrews saw how all the promises were ultimately fulfilled in Christ—in what He has done to provide salvation and what He will do to bring God's plan for earth to fulfillment. Faith is being able to wait and trust the Lord to fulfill all He has said He will do, even if life is hard for us now.

How have people responded to God's delays?

The people of the past have responded as you and I might have. Some grew impatient. Others kept the faith. Still others mocked those who looked to the future.

Abraham had his moments of doubt even though he was a man of faith. When his wife Sarah grew old without bearing a child, Abraham and Sarah began to get creative about fulfilling God's promise. The birth of Ishmael by Hagar was the result (Gen. 16). But God, in His time, brought about the miraculous birth of Isaac (Gen. 21:1-7).

The Hebrews who came out of Egypt complained and griped against Moses and against God because not everything turned out just as they expected after they escaped slavery in Egypt. As a result, they ended up wandering around in the desert for 40 years—and a whole generation of people missed out on the promise of entering Palestine (Num. 14).

David was anointed king while Saul was still on the throne. Yet David was a fugitive from Saul's "hit men" for many years. When he did become king, David saw much evidence of the Lord's goodness to him. But David's kingship was far from tranquil, with betrayals and turmoil (1 Sam. 16–31; 2 Sam. 1–24).

Job came to realize that perfect justice was not to be experienced during our lifetime. He learned that God's timing and God's program are perfect and wise (Job 42).

The disciples had to learn that Jesus was not immediately going to reestablish the nation of Israel and inaugurate the millennial kingdom (Acts 1:6-8). They had to learn that there was going to be a period of time between His first coming and His second coming (Mt. 24–25). Because Jesus was not the conquering king that many people expected, they rejected Him, and only a few believed in Him until after the resurrection.

Paul wrote encouraging words to believers who were in danger of despair in the face of persecution and the prospect of not seeing immediate relief (1 Cor. 15; 2 Cor. 4).

Unbelievers in the last days will ridicule the promise of Christ's second coming. The apostle Peter said that these scoffers would say, "Where is the promise of His coming?" (2 Pet. 3:4). Peter responded with these words:

> *Beloved, do not forget this one thing, that with the Lord one day is as a thousand years, and a thousand years as one day. The Lord is not slack concerning His promise, as some count slackness, but is longsuffering toward us, not willing that any should perish but that all should come to repentance* (2 PET. 3:8-9).

Believers, those who profess faith in Christ as Lord and Savior, have a life that can be far from glorious. We can be plagued with impatience and doubts. Like the psalmist, we may wonder why God allows the wicked to prosper and why He doesn't fulfill His promise by bringing judgment right now (Ps. 73). We too can become so distracted by the present world that we lose sight of the world to come.

We can also benefit from what the apostle Paul wrote at the close of his first letter to Timothy. He warned about a preoccupation with the present— the riches and the pleasure of life. Paul encouraged Timothy to "pursue righteousness, godliness, faith, love, patience, gentleness," and to "fight the good fight of faith" (1 Tim. 6:11-12). The apostle then said about Christ's second coming. "He will manifest [it] in His own time" (v. 15).

Who is wiser than God? Nobody. All of the promises of God are fulfilled in His perfect timing, according to His wisdom. Many of those promises are fulfilled now. Many await fulfillment. All who trust Christ for forgiveness of sins receive that forgiveness and new life immediately— along with all the spiritual benefits (Jn. 3; Eph. 1).

And while some people experience the evidence of God's love and care through prosperity of life and good health, others experience the love and strength of God through poverty and sickness. In all cases, though, God is true to His word. He fulfills His promises.

Thinking It Over
What promises of God would encourage a follower of Christ to keep on living for Him? How do people in the world mock the hope of Christians? What fulfillment of biblical promises can give you and me confidence that God will keep His promises to us now and in the life to come?

Promise Checklist

If you want to follow the advice of the great hymn "Standing On The Promises," you need to be sure you are on solid footing. As we've seen in this study of God's promises, our spiritual lives must be founded on what God has said—not merely on what we wish He had said or what we think He might have said. We need to be sure we are not misquoting the Lord when we claim a biblical promise for ourselves.

The basic rules of proper interpretation that apply to the whole Bible also form the starting point for our interpretation of biblical promises. The rules of interpretation can be summed up in one word—context. Two principles are especially relevant to this study.

The context of immediate setting: Look at the verses that immediately precede and follow the promise. Does your interpretation fit the context?

The context of the whole Bible: Consider the passage in its relation to the whole Bible. God does not contradict Himself. The interpretation of the promise must be in keeping with all of Scripture. This step requires a growing knowledge of God's Word and a dependence on the Holy Spirit to guide your understanding of the Bible.

In this chapter we have examined the promises of God in four categories. As we read the Scriptures, we can learn how to interpret and apply those promises.

Use the questions listed here as guidelines.

1. The *terms* of the promise.

Does the promise have conditions to fulfill?
Do you meet the conditions?
What will happen if you fail to measure up?
What characteristics of God can increase your confidence in His promises?

2. The *people* of the promise.

Is the promise given to all people of all time?
Is a specific individual mentioned?
Are only believers in view?
Is the promise to obedient believers only?
Are you included?

3. The *method* of the promise.

Does the Scripture imply obvious fulfillment?
Could the promise be fulfilled spiritually?
Could the promise be fulfilled physically?
How is God's faithfulness demonstrated?
What are some of the options in your situation?

4. The *time* of the promise.

Can fulfillment be expected soon?
Will it be fulfilled in heaven?
Can God fulfill this promise a number of times?
Why would God possibly delay fulfillment?
Are you willing to trust God's timing?
Could the promise be only partially fulfilled?

Too Good
To Be True?

In the world of shopping, if the product sounds
too good to be true, it probably is. Whether it's
a vegetable chopper, a weed whacker, or the latest
automobile, the advertised image is more likely to
be a mirage than reality. What you think is a bar-
gain can turn out to be a major disappointment.

God never advertises more than He delivers. He's
not out to deceive us. He wants us to have the best
He has to offer—the joy of a close relationship with
Him now, and heaven later.

To enjoy God's best, though, you and I first need
to take Jesus at His word. He said, "He who hears
My word and believes in Him who sent Me has ever-

lasting life, and shall not come into judgment, but has passed from death into life" (Jn. 5:24).

His offer is conditioned only on our acceptance of His free gift. Does it sound too easy? Too good to be true? It's not. Jesus has proven that He can be trusted. He came to earth, lived a perfect life, died on the cross in our place, and rose from the dead. If He can't be trusted, nobody can.

If you've never done so, choose now to take God at His word. Admit that you deserve God's judgment for sin, believe Jesus died for you and rose from the dead, accept His offer of new life, and then build your life on the promises of God.